W9-AZJ-672

The American Revolution

By
GEORGE LEE

COPYRIGHT © 1996 Mark Twain Media, Inc.

ISBN   10-digit: 1-58037-010-1
        13-digit: 978-1-58037-010-3

Printing No. CD-1887

Mark Twain Media, Inc., Publishers
Distributed by Carson-Dellosa Publishing Company, Inc.

Do Ben Franklin's Propaganda Sheet.

TABLE OF CONTENTS

Colonial and Revolutionary America Time Line iii

Introduction 1

The First Inhabitants of North America 2

The First Colonies North of Mexico 6

Plymouth and Massachusetts Bay 10

New Colonies Planted in the North 14

Settling the Southern Colonies 18

Religion in the Colonies 22

The Colonial Economy 26

Social Status in the Colonies 30

Slavery in the Colonies 34

Young People's Lives in the Colonies 38

Colonial Clothing 42

The New Man (and Woman) 46

The Head Under the Crown 50

Government in the Colonies 54

New France 58

Wars Come to North America 62

Beginnings of Conflict (1763–1766) 66

New Taxes and a Massacre (1766–1770) 70

George III & Company 74

Adams, Henry, and Paine 78

Boston's Tea Party (1771–1774) 82

Declaring Independence (1774–1776) 86

Washington: Symbol of the Revolution 90

Weighing the Odds 94

Early Stages of the War (1776–1777) 98

The Diplomatic War 102

The Naval War 106

The Road to Yorktown 110

The Confederation 114

Constitutional Convention 118

The Constitution They Wrote 122

Ratification and a New Republic 126

Colonial Times Crossword Puzzle 130

Answer Keys 131

Bibliography 139

COLONIAL AND REVOLUTIONARY AMERICA
TIME LINE

Time lines are useful tools for keeping events in the proper sequence. *Italicized* dates are events that helped to shape Colonial and Revolutionary America indirectly. Book titles and names of ships are also italicized.

1497	John Cabot's exploration.
1519–21	Cortes conquers Mexico.
1519–22	*Magellan's crew sails around the world.*
1524	French explorer, Verrazano, reaches New York and Narragansett Bay.
1527–36	Narvaez expedition into Florida.
1540–42	Coronado explores the southwest for Spain.
1587–90	Roanoke Island colony is planted and disappears.
1588	*Battle of the Spanish Armada.*
1603	*Elizabeth I dies; James I succeeds her.*
1607	Jamestown colony established; beginning of Virginia settlement.
1614	Dutch plant New Netherland colony on Manhattan Island.
1619	Virginia allowed representative government; slaves enter Virginia.
1620	Plymouth colony established.
1625	*James I dies; Charles I succeeds him.*
1630	Massachusetts Bay Colony established.
1632	Maryland charter granted to Lord Baltimore.
1635	Connecticut settlement begins.
1636	Harvard College established.
1637	Pequot War ends Indian threat to New Englanders.
1642–49	*English Civil War ends in Cromwell's Commonwealth.*
1644	Rhode Island's charter granted.
1649	Maryland Toleration Act.
1664	English take New Netherland colony, rename it New York.
1651	*Parliament passes first Navigation Act.*
1660	*Monarchy restored; Charles II assumes throne.*
1663	Carolina charter granted.
1675	King Philip's War in New England.
1676	Bacon's Rebellion in Virginia.
1679	New Hampshire chartered as royal colony.
1681	William Penn receives title to Pennsylvania.
1682	Penn authorized to rule Delaware. LaSalle claims Louisiana for France.
1685	*Charles II dies; James II replaces him.*
1688	*James II ousted and replaced by William and Mary.*
1689–97	*King William's War.*
1692	Witchcraft trials in Salem, Massachusetts.
1702–13	*Queen Anne's War.*
1704	First regular colonial newspaper, *The Boston News-Letter,* published.
1732	Georgia charter granted.

1734	Great Awakening begins in Massachusetts.
1735	Zenger trial in New York ends in victory for freedom of the press.
1744–48	*King George's War.*
1747	Benjamin Franklin's *Poor Richard's Almanack* is first published.
1754	Washington's effort to convince French to leave Virginia soil fails.
1755	Braddock expedition ends in failure.
1756–63	*Seven Years War begins in Europe.* (French and Indian War in the colonies.)
1759	Wolfe captures Quebec for England.
1760	Montreal falls to English.
1763	France loses its empire in North America. Proclamation Line drawn.
1764	Sugar Act passed to enforce taxes on imported sugar.
1765	Stamp Act passed by Parliament. Stamp Act Congress meets. Quartering Act requires colonists to house British troops. Sons of Liberty formed.
1766	Stamp Act repealed and Declaratory Act passed.
1767	Townshend Acts put tax on tea, glass, paper, and so forth.
1768	British troops are sent to Boston.
1770	Boston Massacre.
1772	Revenue ship *Gaspee* is sunk. Committees of Correspondence begin operations.
1773	Tea Act. Boston Tea Party.
1774	Coercive [Intolerable] Acts passed. Parliament passes Quebec Act. First Continental Congress meets.
1775	Battles of Lexington and Concord. Second Continental Congress meets. Battle of Breed's [better known as Battle of Bunker] Hill. George III declares that the colonies are in rebellion.
1776	Thomas Paine's *Common Sense* is published. British troops leave Boston. Declaration of Independence. British take New York City.
1776–77	Battles of Trenton and Princeton.
1777	British take Philadelphia. British invasion under St. Leger fails to take western New York. Burgoyne defeated at Saratoga. French Alliance is signed.
1777–78	Washington's army at Valley Forge.
1778	Savannah falls to British.
1780	Charleston falls to British.
1781	Cornwallis surrenders at Yorktown. Articles of Confederation approved.
1783	Newburgh Conspiracy. Peace treaty with England is signed.
1785	Land Ordinance approved by Confederation Congress. Jay-Gardoqui Treaty rejected by Congress.
1786	Annapolis Convention. Shays' Rebellion.
1787	Constitutional Convention. Northwest Ordinance.
1789	Constitution ratified by nine states. Washington takes oath of office as first President of the United States.

INTRODUCTION

To the first Asian hunters who crossed into Alaska and moved southward into a continent just recovering from the ice age, the land looked no different from what they had left behind. To the early European explorers, it was just a barrier blocking their passage to Asia. It took time for the resources and wealth of this new world to be discovered and even longer for its value as a land offering the opportunity to shed the past to be appreciated.

Between the lands of the King of France and the King of Spain were the British colonies, a territory acting as a magnet to draw the religious minorities, the poor, and the ambitious who either chose to or were forced to come. Not all were English, and from the beginning, mixtures of nationalities were present. By 1700 German, Dutch, French, Swedish, Spanish, and a host of native languages were spoken in the 13 colonies.

During this time, many colorful and outstanding people lived in the colonies. There were the courageous like Pocahontas and Captain John Smith, the religious like William Bradford and Jonathan Edwards, slaves like Phillis Wheatley and Crispus Attucks, the wise like Benjamin Franklin and Thomas Jefferson, the outspoken like Patrick Henry and James Otis, clever shapers of public opinion like Sam Adams and Thomas Paine, and those driven by a sense of duty like George Washington and John Adams. On occasion, we honor them. We remember the Pilgrims on Thanksgiving and the signers of the Declaration of Independence on the Fourth of July. The other 363 days of the year, however, their images sit quietly in the corner of our minds.

But they were important in shaping the nation we became. They gave us the language we speak, the ideals of freedom we cherish, and the belief that a person can and should take advantage of opportunities. They taught the values of hard work, resourcefulness, and education. We can concede that they had faults without taking away from their achievements. This book is about people who lived hundreds of years ago, but whose tradition is part of our lives today.

—THE AUTHOR—

THE FIRST INHABITANTS OF NORTH AMERICA

Who discovered America? Most historians say it was Columbus in 1492. The Scandinavians claim it was Leif Ericson in 1003. But ahead of the Europeans by many centuries was a stone age hunter and his family who crossed the land bridge between Alaska and Siberia in search of food. Who he was and when he came no one knows for sure, but we know that others followed him and, centuries later, descendants could be found in North, Central, and South America and on islands of the Caribbean. Some of those descendants developed great civilizations that built large structures and devised written languages and calendars. Others became farmers using primitive tools. Still others continued to hunt.

Native civilizations were thriving in the Americas centuries before European explorers arrived.

Europeans who came later met their descendants. The Norse called them "Skrellings," Columbus called them "Indians," and anthropologists said they were "Amerinds"; in the late twentieth century they became "Native Americans." These natives gave their peoples various names: Incas in Peru and Aztecs and Mayas in Mexico. In North America, they chose hundreds of names to describe their people. From those have come the names of states, counties, cities, rivers, and lakes within the boundaries of what is now the United States. Since this book is primarily about the region east of the Mississippi River, our study of native culture concentrates on that area.

LANGUAGE. We do not know if the "natives" ever had a common language, but if they did, it was lost as groups moved farther away from each other and were separated by mountains, rivers, and lakes. Still, there was enough contact between those in the same region that "language groups" made it possible to communicate. In the area east of the Mississippi River, there were four of these. Algonquian was spoken by coastal tribes from Canada to Virginia. Its usage was common among tribes from the coast west to the upper Mississippi River region and to central Canada. Iroquois was the language used by the tribes clustered around the Great Lakes and a few tribes further south. Siouan was much more common west of the river than in the East, but there were small areas east of the river where it was the language of choice. From South Carolina to the southern tip of Florida and across to the lower Mississippi valley, Gulf languages were spoken.

ORGANIZATION. The largest unit in native culture was the tribe. Membership in the tribe was like citizenship; the child was born into it, and the tribe's name carried special meaning. "Cherokee" meant "cave people" or "real people." "Pequot" meant "destroyers." "Mohawk" meant "they eat live things." "Seneca" meant "people of the rocks." Tribes might join in a federation like the Iroquois League made up of five nations or the Powhatan Confederation of 200 Algonquin villages in Virginia.

2

Clan. The major division within the tribe, it was made up of people often related to each other and was usually represented by an animal (totem). The head of the clan in most tribes was the oldest woman, who had great power and influence. Membership in the clan was on the mother's side, not the father's. People could not marry inside their clans. The clans took care of their own and punished anyone harming a clan member.

Family structure was very complex. Husband and wife belonged to different clans and kept their clan tie after marriage. The fireside family (father, mother, children) was the most basic unit. In some tribes, they lived in separate homes; in others, they lived with other families.

HOUSING differed from tribe to tribe. The Iroquois "long houses" were 50 to 100 feet long and 16 to 18 feet wide. The interior was divided into compartments, and a hole in the bark-covered roof released the smoke. Virginia and North Carolina tribes preferred a round, oblong style of long house.

VIEW OF PROPERTY. Property questions caused much trouble between the races. The natives believed land was like water or air—there for everyone. When whites offered money or gifts for land, they took it, with the same wonder that you or I would if someone offered to pay us for air. Tribes claimed land but did not divide it up or give it to individuals to use forever. Europeans, of course, could hold title to land or exchange it with a signature on a contract.

FIRST CONTACTS WITH WHITES. Early contact between the races almost always resulted in tragedy for someone. When Thorwald Ericson (brother of Leif) came in A.D. 1006, he took eight natives prisoner and killed them. Ponce de León sailed to Florida in 1513 and fought the people of the first village he entered. He left the east coast, went to the west coast of the penninsula, and battled the natives he met there. Ponce waited until 1521 to return, and this time he was fatally wounded by an arrow.

The Narvaez expedition in 1527 found their reception in Florida to be similar to Ponce de León's. After robbing and burning villages, they were trailed by tough warriors who carried bows seven feet long and could hit a target at 200 paces. Narvaez escaped in a boat into the Gulf of Mexico, leaving some of his men behind to take care of themselves. One of those, Cabeza de Vaca, made it back to Mexico after many adventures with the natives.

Hernando de Soto's expedition was much longer and undoubtedly left an impression on the natives. Landing at Tampa Bay in 1538, he brought large hunting dogs ashore that were trained to attack natives. He burned villages, took hostages, and held natives in chain gangs. De Soto's journey did bring one positive thing to the natives: hogs that thrived on native corn and in time became the famous razorbacks.

Activity

Europeans have come to your village (classroom) and want to buy it. Hold a discussion among the "native" students about whether to accept the beads being offered and the "European" students about the terms of the sale.

Name_____ Date_____

POINTS TO PONDER

1. What conditions might cause some natives to be farmers, others hunters, and still others builders and craftsmen?

_____

_____

_____

_____

2. To what extent are professional sport names and school athletic team names like totems? Try to develop a mythical history for your school's athletic team's name.

_____

_____

_____

_____

3. Suppose your family lived in a long house with nine other families. How would it be different from your current lifestyle?

_____

_____

_____

_____

4. How would you account for the way Europeans treated the natives?

_____

_____

_____

_____

Name_____ Date_____

CHALLENGES

1. Who do Scandinavians believe discovered America?

_____

2. What were two signs that native civilization was advancing?

_____

_____

3. Who refer to Native Americans as Amerinds?

_____

4. Which group of native languages was used over the largest area east of the Mississippi River?

_____

5. Which group of languages was used most around the Great Lakes?

_____

6. Which tribe had the reputation of being destroyers?

_____

7. What was usually the symbol of the clan?

_____

8. What were the natives' opinions of Ponce de Leon?

_____

_____

9. How did de Soto offend the natives?

_____

_____

10. What descendant of the de Soto expedition became famous?

_____

THE FIRST COLONIES NORTH OF MEXICO

After the failure of de Soto and Coronado to find natives who owned gold and silver, the Spanish gave up on the region north of Mexico and planted a few outposts like St. Augustine (1565) to keep raiders away. The region to the north was open for others to explore and colonize. France and England became the main competitors for the region, but both moved cautiously.

FRANCE. In 1535 Jacques Cartier sailed to the St. Lawrence River and named the region New France (Canada). It wasn't until the next century that the French began settling New France. In 1608, Samuel de Champlain established Quebec and made

French and English explorers laid claims to land in the New World for their respective countries.

allies of the Huron (Algonquian). In 1609, he joined a Huron raiding party into Iroquois country where he killed two Mohawks with his musket. That incident turned the Iroquois against France.

ENGLAND. The first to sail west for England was an Italian, John Cabot, who explored the Maine and Nova Scotia coastlines in 1497. Sailing westward again in 1498, Cabot was lost at sea.

By the end of the next century, interest in establishing a North American colony was increasing. Two writers had encouraged the interest. Sir Thomas More's book, *Utopia* (1516), told of a mythical island in the New World where an ideal society might exist. Richard Hakluyt, a Protestant minister and geographer, wrote books urging colonization to accomplish five goals: (1) extend Protestantism, (2) expand trade, (3) increase England's markets, (4) reduce unemployment, and (5) provide bases to attack Spanish ships in case of war.

SIR HUMPHREY GILBERT, a friend of Queen Elizabeth I, was given permission to establish a colony in North America. Colonists were guaranteed all the rights of any English subject. His efforts to establish a colony in Newfoundland in 1583 failed. After Gilbert's death, his half-brother, SIR WALTER RALEIGH, continued the effort and established a colony on Roanoke Island, off North Carolina, in 1585, but the settlers did not stay. In 1587 new settlers went to the island. The intention was to send supplies the next year, but war with Spain interfered, and it was not until 1590 that a supply ship returned. Its crew found the colony deserted, and mystery has existed ever since about the fate of the "Lost Colony."

Raleigh was accused of high treason by King James I, and his rights to establish a colony were given to the Virginia Company of London (London Company). Hoping to find gold and diamonds, they sent 100 colonists in 1607 to establish a settlement on the coast of Virginia.

JAMESTOWN. In honor of the king, they named the colony Jamestown. The 100 men spent their time looking for gold and jewels on the beach. They neglected details like planting crops and building shelters and defenses. This settlement faced destruction until Captain John Smith arrived. Smith was a soldier of fortune who had fought the Turks and had been enslaved by them. After killing his master, Smith fled to Russia and returned to England in 1604. The company gave Smith control of the colony, and he came down hard. His policy was "no work, no food."

Smith's relations with the Indians were interesting. Of native religion, he wrote: "Their chief God they worship is the Devil. Him they call *Oke* and serve him more out of fear than love." Chief Powhatan was the wise ruler of the local tribes. His younger brother, Opechancanough, hated the English intruders and captured Smith. As Smith was about to be killed, Powhatan's favorite daughter, Pocahontas, pled with her father to save him. Smith was released. After Smith returned to Jamestown, Opechancanough refused to sell food to the settlement; Smith took some men to Opechancanough's camp, grabbed the chief by his hair and took him hostage. To save him, the Indians brought supplies in many boats to Jamestown. After his release, Opechancanough's hatred for the English settlers grew. However, Powhatan kept his brother under control.

In 1609, Smith was injured in a gunpowder explosion and returned to England. That same year, the company appointed Lord De La Warr (Delaware) as governor, and he sent Sir Thomas Gates to rule until he arrived. Gates was shipwrecked in Bermuda, but 400 other settlers made it. Without leadership, the men suffered illness, hunger, and lack of organization.

When Gates and his 60 men arrived on little boats they had built in Bermuda, only 60 settlers were still alive. In 1610, Lord Delaware also came and built a settlement upstream at Henrico (Richmond).

Delaware left Gates in charge in 1611, and he ruled with an iron hand. The colony began to grow. In 1612 John Rolfe's blend of West Indian tobacco with that used by natives paid off in a profitable crop that could be sold in England. In 1613, Pocahontas was kidnapped by the settlers, which would have brought war with Powhatan had not Rolfe married her. After she bore a son, Pocahontas went with Rolfe to England, where she quickly became a celebrity. After her death, Rolfe returned to Virginia.

In 1619, two important developments occurred in Virginia. The company decided to allow them to form a legislature that, with the governor, was to rule the colony. That same year, a passing Dutch ship sold 20 blacks to the settlers. Thus, democracy and slavery came in the same year.

Opechancanough became chief after Powhatan's death and carefully plotted his revenge on the English colonists. Without warning, the Indians attacked in 1622, killing 347 settlers, including John Rolfe. James I then decided it was time to remove the charter from the London Company and made Virginia a royal colony in 1624. He planned to take power away from the legislature, but his death in 1625 saved representative government.

Activity

Arrange a CNN interview in England after John Rolfe and Pocahontas arrive in London.

Name_____ Date_____

POINTS TO PONDER

1. If you were going to create a utopian society, what elements of our society would you keep, and what would you drop?

_____

_____

_____

_____

_____

2. How might a lack of organization lead to disaster for colonists in a place like Jamestown?

_____

_____

_____

_____

_____

3. An old saying is that first impressions make a big difference. Would the incidents mentioned in this chapter tend to prove or disprove this statement? Give examples.

_____

_____

_____

_____

_____

Name_____Date_____

CHALLENGES

1. What name did Cartier give to the region we call Canada?

_____

2. How did Champlain's friendship with Algonquians hurt his relations with the Iroquois?

_____

_____

3. We sometimes use the word utopian. What would a utopia be?

_____

_____

4. Hakluyt listed five goals for colonies. What three goals had to do with improving the English economy?

_____

_____

5. Why weren't supplies sent to the Roanoke colony in 1588?

_____

_____

6. For whom was Jamestown named?

_____

7. With which native did Captain John Smith have the most trouble?

_____

8. Who saved Smith's life?

_____

9. What crop did Rolfe plant that saved the colony's economy?

_____

10. What two institutions came to the colony in 1619?

_____

_____

PLYMOUTH AND MASSACHUSETTS BAY

To understand the settlement of New England, one has to go back to religious controversies that began during the reign of Henry VIII. Angered by the Pope's refusal to grant him a divorce, Henry VIII separated the English church from the Roman Catholic Church. The new Church of England (commonly referred to as Anglican) kept many Catholic rituals.

Calvinism came to England from Europe at about the same time. Calvinists opposed Catholic rituals. Those who favored purifying the church of its Catholicism were "Puritans." Those believing it was better to depart and form their own church

Governor John Winthrop wrote the charter for the Massachusetts Bay Colony.

were "Separatists." Of these, Separatists were the more radical. They believed in individuals' rights to worship God in their own way. Calvinists were hard to persuade. Branding, flogging, or imprisonment only made them more stubborn. Elizabeth I was hard on them; James I made them miserable. The Separatists decided to leave. They moved to Holland from 1607–1609, were unhappy there, and began looking toward Virginia. The London Company gave them permission to settle in Virginia, and James I, eager to move them as far away as possible, agreed.

In 1620, 100 would-be settlers and 50 crew members boarded the little *Mayflower*. Not all the passengers were Separatists, and during the voyage, trouble broke out between the groups of travelers. The Pilgrims (as the Separatists called themselves) worried that some of the wild young men might cause trouble when they reached land. Before landing, 41 adults signed the MAYFLOWER COMPACT and agreed to obey whatever laws should be passed for the general good of the colony. They chose Deacon John Carver as governor, but he died in April 1621, and William Bradford replaced him. For 30 of the next 35 years, Bradford governed the colony.

The land they settled was outside that given to the London Company and had been given to the Council of New England (formerly the Plymouth Company). Naming their colony "Plymouth," they began the hard task of turning the rocky and not very fertile land into farms. Their first year would have been their last were it not for Squanto, an English-speaking Wampanoag, who helped establish friendly relations with the tribe. In gratitude for their help, the settlers held a harvest feast with the natives in the fall. The colony never drew many settlers, and when it merged with Massachusetts Bay Colony in 1691, it still had fewer than 1,000 residents.

Of the residents, none gave the Pilgrims more trouble than Thomas Morton, owner of Merrymount. Unlike the Pilgrims, he enjoyed the natives' company and traded them guns and liquor for furs. His merry band had a May Pole where they danced and sang songs that were offensive to the pious settlers. In 1627 Captain Miles Standish (whom Morton called

"Captain Shrimp") arrived with an armed force, arrested him, and sent him to England. He returned in 1630, was arrested, and this time his property was seized and his house was burned. Again, he was exiled to England. He returned to Plymouth in 1645 and was ordered to leave. Going to Boston, he was jailed for a year, then released. He never gave them any more trouble.

MASSACHUSETTS BAY. Along the New England coastline, small fishing villages were being constructed in the 1620s. One of these villages, Cape Ann, was backed by a group of Puritans from Dorchester, England. Two motives for establishing a colony drove them: (1) economic, and (2) religious. In Puritanism, the two became one, because they believed God prospered those who best served him. Puritans were hard-working people.

The two men most important in establishing a colony were Reverend John White (who wanted a Christian mission to the natives and fishermen) and a devout Puritan lawyer, John Winthrop (who realized that royal persecution of the Puritans was increasing). Winthrop wrote the charter establishing the colony. A very important detail was left out: it did not say that the colony's meetings were to be held in England. None of the king's advisors caught that detail, and the king approved it. All company board members migrated to the colony. The charter granted to the Bay colonists gave them the power to rule the land under their control. They would elect a governor, deputy governor, and 18 assistants. These officers were to be picked by the "freemen" (males meeting voting qualifications) four times a year.

In March 1630, the *Arbella,* carrying Governor Winthrop and the charter, along with six other ships, sailed to Massachusetts. They were followed by more ships carrying 1,000 settlers. Boston quickly became their most important city and soon attracted thousands more.

The founders of the Bay Colony had a sense of purpose in what they were doing. On the way over, Governor Winthrop told them they were building "a city upon a hill," a godly community setting an example. In this community, none were to prosper at the expense of others. All would be reasonably poor together. They were short on cash, but not on food. Game was plentiful: large turkeys and deer were within gun range, and fish were just off shore.

They were also interested in educating their young people. Harvard College was established in 1636 with a grant of £800 from the legislature and the library from William Harvard's estate. Grammar schools stressing Latin and Greek were started. To stop Satan from keeping "men from the knowledge of the Scriptures," a 1647 law ordered towns with 50 or more families to appoint a schoolmaster. Towns of 100 families were to open a grammar school. Massachusetts became a center for education, and other New England colonies followed their example.

Activity

If you were going to establish a colony in the 1600s, considering the difficulty of getting supplies across the ocean, make a list of the major items you would bring with you.

11

Name_____Date_____

POINTS TO PONDER

1. Why kinds of problems do you think the Separatists might have run into in Holland? (Think about the problems *you* would have living in a foreign country).

_____

_____

_____

_____

_____

2. Why would someone like Morton draw so much attention from the Calvinist authorities in Plymouth and Massachusetts?

_____

_____

_____

_____

_____

_____

3. Why was it important that the Massachusetts charter be with the leaders of the new colony and not in England?

_____

_____

_____

_____

_____

Name_____Date_____

CHALLENGES

1. Why was the name "Puritan" used to describe one group of Calvinists?

_____

_____

2. Why was "Separatist" used to describe another Calvinist group?

_____

_____

3. What was the effect of punishing them?

_____

_____

4. Who was the long-time governor of Plymouth colony?

_____

5. By what name was the old "Virginia Company of Plymouth" now known?

_____

6. What holiday do you think came out of the Plymouth harvest feast?

_____

7. How did Thomas Morton offend the Pilgrims?

_____

_____

8. What important detail was not included in the Bay colony's charter?

_____

_____

9. Why was food not a serious problem in the Massachusetts Bay colony?

_____

_____

10. What two languages were stressed in grammar schools?

_____

NEW COLONIES PLANTED IN THE NORTH

New colonies were planted along the shores of North America. Some were labelled "royal," meaning the governor was appointed by the king; some were "proprietary," with governors appointed by the proprietor; "charter" colonies elected their governor and legislature. In the northern region of the British American colonies, all three types existed.

William Penn allowed religious freedom in his Pennsylvania Colony.

CONNECTICUT. In 1635 groups of settlers from Massachusetts built communities along the Connecticut River. The main force behind this immigration was Reverend Thomas Hooker, who believed "the foundation of authority is laid in the free exercise of the people." In 1637 the Pequot War broke out, and the colony's future was in danger, but Connecticut troops led by John Mason destroyed the Pequot's stronghold.

Residents of the three Connecticut towns wrote the Fundamental Orders, the first written constitution in history. The governor and six assistants were elected by a majority of those meeting voting requirements.

RHODE ISLAND. Roger Williams, a Cambridge University graduate, arrived in Plymouth in 1631 and went from there to Salem, Massachusetts, to become minister of the church in 1633. He strongly disagreed with Bay Colony leaders on a number of topics. He favored separation of church and state; he opposed making people go to church and using tax money to support the church. He said land should be bought from the natives, not given away by the king. In 1636 the Massachusetts General Court ordered Williams to leave; the next spring he went to Narragansett Bay and established Providence Plantation, the beginning of the colony of Rhode Island.

A committee of Parliament approved a charter drawn up by the colonists in 1644. Because of the religious freedom present in the colony from the beginning, Rhode Island attracted persecuted people. Anne Hutchinson's quarrel with Puritan leaders in Massachusetts caused her to go there. Jews and Quakers were accepted there when no one else wanted them. The bickering in the colony between religious and political factions, however, made other colonies glad for their strict policies toward agitators.

NEW HAMPSHIRE. Settlements north of Massachusetts developed as early as 1623; some were formed by religious groups, and others were motivated by economic opportunity. In 1629 John Mason received a large land grant and named it New Hampshire. The settlers he brought in were mostly Anglican farmers and fishermen. After his death, the towns were left to take care of their own affairs. New Hampshire became a royal colony in 1679.

NEW YORK. Henry Hudson, an English sailor employed by the Dutch East India Company, sailed up what became the Hudson River on the *Half Moon* in 1609. His report on the region encouraged the company to open a fur trade with the Iroquois. In 1614, the Dutch colony of New Netherland was planted from Manhattan Island up the Hudson River to Albany. Governor Peter Minuit bought Manhattan Island from the natives for 60 guilders ($24).

The most important governor of the colony was Peter Stuyvesant, who governed from 1647 to 1664. Wearing a peg leg, he ruled the colony in a high-handed but effective way. He made many improvements: straightening streets, building a canal, and building a wall north of the city to protect it from Indian attack (Wall Street is located there today).

The British were unhappy to see this prospering colony in foreign hands. Charles II claimed England had discovered the region and gave his brother, the Duke of York, title to it in 1664. A British fleet sailed to New Amsterdam, and it surrendered without a fight. The transition from Dutch to English rule went smoothly, and the Dutch were allowed to keep their large estates (patroonships) along the Hudson River.

NEW JERSEY. After receiving title to New York, the Duke of York gave his lands between the Hudson and Delaware rivers to George Carteret (former governor of the Isle of Jersey) and Lord Berkeley. A few Swedish, Dutch, and English settlers were already there. Berkeley had so many problems that he sold his land to Quakers for £1,000; Carteret sold his later. New Jersey residents were given freedom of conscience, trial by jury, and no taxation without approval of representatives in 1677.

PENNSYLVANIA was given to William Penn by Charles II in 1681, either as payment for a debt owed his father or as a gift of friendship. Penn was a Quaker. Quakers had many enemies in most colonies. Penn referred to his colony as a "Holy Experiment," with religious freedom to all who believed in God and fair treatment to natives. He bought land from natives, saw that they were treated justly in courts, and even learned the Delaware language. For poor whites, Pennsylvania offered great opportunities. A man could buy 100 acres for £2. Penn's system of law allowed only two hanging offenses, trial by jury, and sentences to reform the guilty.

Penn was good at advertising his colony, and it drew a variety of nationalities: Swedes, Germans, Dutch, Scots-Irish and Welsh. So many Germans came that others called them "Pennsylvania Dutch" (*Deutsch* is the proper name for the German language). Many types of religious groups were attracted: Quakers, Lutherans, Presbyterians, Moravians, and others. The Quaker influence was strongest, however. The most important men in town were almost always Quakers. Vices offending Quakers became illegal: gambling, dancing, drunkenness, stage plays, and novels were forbidden.

DELAWARE. In 1682 Penn was authorized to rule Delaware. At first, Delaware was considered part of Pennsylvania, but it was allowed its own legislature in 1701, although Pennsylvania's governor was also Delaware's.

Activity

Make a list of the different guarantees of freedoms in northern colonies. Decide which were the more important later when the Bill of Rights was added to the Constitution.

Name_____Date_____

POINTS TO PONDER

1. You are thinking about moving to the colonies, but you are not sure which one. Would the type of government make a difference in your choice? Why?

_____

_____

_____

_____

_____

2. Which northern colonies seemed to allow the most freedom? Which seemed to have less?

_____

_____

_____

_____

3. Which colonies seemed to have the most diverse (different groups) population? What drew them to that colony?

_____

_____

_____

_____

_____

Name_____ Date_____

CHALLENGES

1. Who selected the governor in a royal colony?

_____

2. How was the governor chosen in a charter colony?

_____

_____

3. Which of the three general types of colonies was Connecticut?

_____

4. Who did Reverend Hooker believe should choose the leaders?

_____

5. Why was Roger Williams forced out of Massachusetts?

_____

_____

6. Describe the people that John Mason brought into New Hampshire.

_____

_____

7. What famous land deal did Minuit make?

_____

_____

8. What two men were important in the early days of New Jersey?

_____

9. What was the most prominent group in early Pennsylvania?

_____

10. What was unusual about the governor of Delaware?

_____

_____

SETTLING THE SOUTHERN COLONIES

Like those to the north, southern colonies drew settlers with a wide variety of backgrounds. A few wealthy aristocrats came, but most were small farmers and workers with an ambition to accomplish more than was possible in their homelands. Aside from Virginia, four other southern colonies were established along the coast.

MARYLAND. Roman Catholics were no more popular in England than Puritans, and a prominent Catholic, George Calvert (Lord Baltimore) wanted to create a colony where his people could freely practice their religion. He was friendly with Charles I and in 1632 was granted the land north of Virginia and bordering it at the Potomac River. Lord Baltimore never went to Maryland, but instead governed it through his brother, Leonard Calvert.

James Oglethorpe established the colony of Georgia hoping that those in England's debtors prisons could be given a second chance to make a good life.

Maryland was a colony badly divided within itself. The "haves" were the planter friends of the Calverts who were given large grants of land. They in turn leased (rented) land to farmers (the have-nots). Everyone had to pay a "quit-rent" (tax) to the proprietor. Leonard Calvert had all the power; he was general, admiral, chief justice, and appointer of all other officials. An assembly was elected, but he could dissolve it (stop it from meeting). The have-nots were very unhappy since they were Protestants, over-taxed, and envious of their planter neighbors and landlords.

To stop some of the arguing over religion and to prove he treated the Protestants fairly, Lord Baltimore approved the Maryland Toleration Act in 1649. Anyone believing in the divinity of Jesus Christ was free to practice their religion in Maryland. Any person bothering a person practicing their faith was to be fined, and if they did not pay, they would be publicly whipped or imprisoned until the proprietor or governor released them.

Maryland had serious boundary problems with Delaware and Pennsylvania. The Pennsylvania boundary dispute was settled when two English mathematicians, Charles Mason and Jeremiah Dixon, established the line between the colonies in 1767. This Mason-Dixon line became famous later as the separating line dividing slave states from free states.

SOUTH CAROLINA. Charles I gave Sir Robert Heath a grant he called "Carolana" in 1629, but after Heath did nothing with it, the offer was cancelled. In 1663 Charles II gave the same land (including North and South Carolina and Georgia) to eight lords proprietor. Settlers finally arrived in 1671. The first job of any colony was to survive, and that was the challenge faced by South Carolina's early settlers. Time and effort went into clearing land, planting crops, and building forts and homes.

In 1680 the new town of Charleston was established on the Ashley River. Unlike earlier settlements at Boston and New York, Charleston was built with straight streets, usually meeting at right angles. Twenty years later, South Carolina's population was still small, but the colony was attracting a variety of immigrants, including French Protestant Huguenots. The first slaves arrived about 1700.

After experimenting with other crops, South Carolina turned to rice as its basic crop. Meat was plentifully supplied by turkeys, cattle, hogs, and fish. Cattle, oxen, and horses were easily raised because the climate was so warm that no fodder had to be set aside for the winter.

NORTH CAROLINA. After the experience of the Lost Colony (1587–90), there were no settlers in North Carolina until the 1650s, when Virginians began to move into the area north of Albemarle Sound. Part of "Carolana" in 1629, all of Carolina was ruled as one colony until 1712, when the proprietors appointed a separate governor for the northern part of the grant.

Growth came slowly to North Carolina. It was not until 1706 that a town was incorporated there (Bath), and another four years lapsed before New Bern was founded. Several problems slowed the growth process. In 1711 after the usually peaceful Tuscarora Indians protested whites seizing their lands and selling their people as slaves, the Tuscarora War broke out. After losing the war, the Tuscarora moved to New York and became the sixth nation of the Iroquois Confederation.

In its early days, the colony was very isolated; the only land route was to Virginia, and it was very difficult. Bigger ships could not cross sandbars along the coast. A few settlers were wealthy, but most were small farmers trying to make a little money selling tobacco and corn, but producing mostly for their own needs. Its isolation also made North Carolina a good hiding place for outlaws, debtors, runaway slaves, and indentured servants escaping from other colonies.

GEORGIA. Georgia came about as the result of James Oglethorpe's concern for inmates of English debtors' prisons. He felt they needed new surroundings and new opportunities. He also wanted to help Protestants in Germany and other parts of Europe. Parliament approved £10,000 (a generous grant), and individuals contributed to a fund to establish a colony. It was named in honor of George II, who granted Oglethorpe and 20 other individuals the lands between the Savannah and Altamaha Rivers in 1732. The first group of 150 settlers arrived the next year.

One reason England wanted this colony established was to protect the Carolinas from Spanish attack. After war broke out between England and Spain in 1739, Oglethorpe unsuccessfully attacked St. Augustine in 1740. In 1742 he defeated a Spanish invasion at Bloody Marsh.

The colony did not turn out exactly the way Oglethorpe expected. Few in debtors' prisons came. He tried to keep slavery out of Georgia, but the people needed workers, and in 1755, slaves arrived in the colony.

Activity

As a reformer, you want to help a group (select some group you feel sorry for) settle vacant land. Assuming you had the finances necessary, what would happen when it came time to bring the group to America?

Name_____ Date_____

POINTS TO PONDER

1. Do you think the Maryland Toleration Act lived up to its title? Why?

_____

_____

_____

_____

_____

2. Look at a map showing the streets of your town. Are they laid out in neat rectangles or are they crooked? What do you think caused that?

_____

_____

_____

_____

_____

3. How does geography play a role in the success or failure of a community or colony (state) to grow?

_____

_____

_____

_____

_____

Name_____ Date_____

CHALLENGES

1. What group did Lord Baltimore want to help?

_____

2. Who benefitted from the quit-rent?

_____

3. Did the Maryland Toleration Act include Jews and atheists? Why?

_____

_____

4. What made Charleston different from other colonial towns?

_____

_____

5. What crop did South Carolina grow to sell?

_____

6. What colony was North Carolina attached to in its early days?

_____

7. What were the main cash crops of colonial North Carolina?

_____

_____

8. Why did North Carolina have a bad reputation?

_____

_____

9. What two groups did James Oglethorpe hope to help?

_____

_____

10. What group did Oglethorpe want to keep out that his settlers wanted to bring in?

_____

RELIGION IN THE COLONIES

Puritans, Anglicans, Quakers, and Catholics disagreed on many issues, but they agreed on one thing: religion was important. Their debates over minor questions of theology were endless, and their refusal to accept any views that disagreed with their own as valid appear strange to us. *Toleration* was not a word in their vocabulary. Many modern people try to be "politically correct," but the early colonists were concerned with being "religiously correct," because eternity was at stake.

It was believed that religion was part of the glue that held the nation together, so in the kingdom of "Acceptability" where "A" was the state religion, tax money paid the salaries of its ministers and contributed to the upkeep of its

Jonathan Edwards helped stir religious enthusiasm in New England during the Great Awakening.

churches. Those belonging to the "B's" were not only "heretics," but disloyal, so the king punished the B's to reform them. The B's were not about to convert to A; they might move to the kingdom of "Belief" (where B's ruled) or start a colony where B was *the* religion. There anyone not a B would then have to live by their rules and pay taxes to support the B church.

In America, religion had to adjust. The people were scattered, so there might not be enough A's or B's to form a church or hire a minister. Or an important C might move to a B colony; should he be denied a voice in the colony's affairs? In time, the majority of Americans did not belong to any church, so they thought it was unfair for any of their money to be going to support the established church. Rhode Island never had an established church. New York allotted tax money to the Dutch Reformed where they were the majority and to Anglicans where they were the majority. It was Puritan Congregationalists in New England and Anglicans in the South who were most successful in keeping tax money flowing to their established churches.

Even where there was an established church, it operated differently in America than in England or Europe. An example was the Anglican church. In England, the priest had his job for life, and his salary was paid directly by the government. In Virginia, the priest was hired from one year to the next, and he was paid by the parish with a specified amount of tobacco. In Europe, the Catholic Church was powerful, but in America, Catholics were a small minority; they wanted freedom of religion in America, as did Baptists, Presbyterians, Moravians, Quakers, and other groups.

SALEM WITCHCRAFT TRIALS. Puritan influence in New England was weakened by the witchcraft trials in Salem, Massachusetts. Even scientists and scholars believed in witches at that time. Without modern medical diagnoses and psychiatry to help understand their actions, strange behavior was explained by the belief that Satan had possessed the individual. In Italy, Spain, France, and Germany, many such "witches" were put to death. In 1661, 120 witches were hanged in England. In 1647–48, an outbreak of witchcraft had been put down in New England, but nothing in North America had happened on the scale of events in Salem, Massachusetts.

The colony was going through hard times: a smallpox epidemic, rising crime, financial depression, and the threat of an Indian uprising. In Salem, a group of girls began behaving in bizarre ways: "flying" around a room with arms outspread, biting their own arms, seeing strange creatures, and interrupting church services. Wild charges accusing unpopular people in the community of being in league with the devil were made by the girls.

The evidence was flimsy, but fear spread. Soon neighbor turned against neighbor, accusing each other of being bewitched. By 1693 everyone knew the whole thing was out of control, and the governor stopped the trials. By that time, 20 people and two dogs had been executed, five were sentenced to death, 150 awaited trial, and 200 others had been accused.

Explanations for the events at Salem vary. Some blame it on bored girls wanting to stir up some activity in town. Others said it was hysteria or ignorance. Some modern research indicates that polluted drinking water affected the behavior of those "possessed."

By 1700 religion seemed out of date. Few attended church. The sermons were very scholarly, and only those who knew Latin, Greek, and Hebrew could follow them. The modern trend was to depend on logic and science for answers to life's problems. Scientific rationalism said the universe ran on its own principles. Deists said there was a God, but He did not interfere with the world's operation.

THE GREAT AWAKENING. In the 1730s religion made a big comeback. Three men were especially important in this. *George Whitefield* (pronounced "Whitfield"), a follower of John Wesley, came to America in 1738 on a speaking tour. He drew huge crowds with his speaking ability; Benjamin Franklin was very impressed by him. *Jonathan Edwards*, minister of the church at Northfield, Massachusetts, felt people had lost sight of God in their desire for money and having a good time. He reminded them that life is short on earth and long in eternity with his famous sermon: "Sinners in the Hands of an Angry God." He brought new religious enthusiasm not only to the town, but to all of New England. *William Tennent* opened the "Log College" to train Presbyterian ministers. Critics attacked their backwoods training, but two graduates later became presidents of Princeton.

By the time of the Revolution, attitudes on religion were much different than those in the 1600s. Protestants were rallying together against threats they felt from deism, rationalism, Catholics, and rumors of an Anglican bishop being appointed for North America. The Great Awakening spread from one colony to another, bringing American colonists closer together.

Activity

Find out more information about the Salem witchcraft trials. What do you think is the most reasonable explanation for the bizarre behavior of those thought to be possessed?

Name_____ Date_____

POINTS TO PONDER

1. Why was religion in trouble by the end of the 17th century?

_____

_____

_____

_____

_____

2. What argument would you have given for an established church if you had been alive at that time? What argument against an established church?

_____

_____

_____

_____

_____

_____

3. A number of famous preachers still hold revivals. How are they alike or different from those of the Great Awakening?

_____

_____

_____

_____

_____

_____

Name_____ Date_____

CHALLENGES

1. In Europe, what attitude did government have toward those who refused to join the official church?

_____

_____

2. What choices did the "B" church have in the "A" nation?

_____

_____

3. What were the two established churches in New York?

_____

4. What was the established church in most southern colonies?

_____

5. What did Catholics and Baptists have in common in America?

_____

_____

6. What was the mood in Massachusetts when trouble began at Salem?

_____

_____

7. By the time it was all over, how many people had been tried or were awaiting trial?

_____

8. Would a deist see any reason to pray? Why?

_____

_____

9. What famous sermon did Jonathan Edwards preach?

_____

10. Who started the Log College?

_____

THE COLONIAL ECONOMY

Making a living in colonial America was hard, back-breaking work, but there were many opportunities for people to start with nothing and become successful.

The settlers who came to America did not come for a vacation. After the "gentlemen" in the first group coming to Virginia realized they were not going to find gold on the beaches, they faced the tasks of getting crops planted and houses built. The Puritans and Quakers farther north thrived on work. To them, idleness was the worst of sins. They believed that those who did not work should not eat, and as Cotton Mather put it: "Refusal to work is a sin against God himself." In the colonies, a person living on relief had to wear a badge with a large "P" for "Pauper" on it.

Unlike England and Europe, where a person might work hard all his life and gain nothing, America offered opportunities for success, and every colony had its examples of poor, hard-working people who, with some luck, made a fortune and spent their old age living in luxury. Only the slaves were denied the opportunity to succeed.

Settlers came from many nations, and they brought their skills with them. The Dutch settlers knew how to make brick and tile so they could build brick homes with tile roofs, as they did in Holland. Swedes brought a different house-building skill with them; they notched logs—the beginning of the log cabin. French Huguenots and Germans brought many skills (weaving, barrel making, gun smithing, leather working, and so forth) that provided needed products for other settlers. Scots played an important part in settling the frontier. Enthusiastic Calvinists, the Scots stressed education. Many colonists from all backgrounds shared the desire that their children be properly educated in Greek and Latin, as well as mathematics. If no local teacher or minister were available to teach their children, they sent them to another town to be instructed.

AGRICULTURE. Most colonists were farmers. They worked with tools that had changed little since Bible times. Most used simple tools: hoes, sickles, and flails. A few had plows, but they were heavy and wooden tipped (farmers believed that iron poisoned the soil). A small garden tiller today cuts deeper and works the ground better than a colonial plow pulled by four oxen and worked by two men. Adding to their problems was that they knew nothing of the value of fertilization, crop rotation, or stock breeding. Scientific farming began around the time of the Revolution.

Food was in plentiful supply. Meat came from wild animals, cattle, fish, chickens, turkeys, and other game birds. Livestock was raised everywhere. Those along the frontier preferred herding hogs and cattle over producing crops, because animals could walk to market instead of being transported. In cities, hogs roamed the streets looking for garbage. Farmers and city dwellers raised gardens of corn, potatos (white and sweet), and other vegetables and fruits. What was grown and sold depended on the climate and soil. New England produced rye, the middle colonies grew wheat, and the southern colonies sold tobacco, rice, and indigo.

WOMEN played a major role in the family's economy. Women made most of the family's clothing, gardened, gathered eggs, milked cows, fed chickens, and made butter, soap, and candles. In their spare time, they cooked, cleaned, washed, and took care of the children.

CHILDREN began doing chores at an early age. Girls worked with their mothers and boys worked with their fathers after reaching three or four years old.

FISHING AND SHIP BUILDING. New England had plenty of trees, poor soil, and great schools of fish offshore. Since farmers had a hard time making a living, working during the winter building ships was helpful. The first American-built ship was produced in 1631; by the end of the century, New England ship-builders had built thousands of ships. These carried people and supplies from England, slaves from the West Indies, and grain and fish to Europe. By 1750 Boston was home port to about 600 ships in foreign commerce and 1,000 ships in coastal trade and fishing. Whaling became a major business in New England when ways were devised to process whale oil on the ship. By the 1770s, 360 ships were involved in searching the oceans for whales. It was a risky but profitable business.

RESTRICTIONS. The British wanted colonies to produce goods that could not be produced in England, but they did not want competition from the colonists. Parliament passed laws called the Navigation Acts to restrict the sale of certain products produced by colonists.

Many Americans needed workers, and there were shortages of skilled laborers. The worker had the economic advantage, but employers controlled the legislatures. Laws were passed to limit wages, but they didn't work because (1) workers were free to go elsewhere, (2) workers would leave that occupation to do something more profitable, or (3) workers would set up shop for themselves. These laws were finally dropped.

TRANSPORTATION. The success of business and economic life depends on a means of getting needed supplies to the consumer. In colonial America, this was done mostly by ship. Even though sailing ships could not guarantee a specified time for arrival, they were faster than land transportation. In most parts of the colonies, there were paths, but no good roads. The only hard surface roads were a few streets in towns; there were none outside the city limits. The first stagecoach line did not open until 1732.

Most overland travel was by horseback, but time lost looking for places to ford streams, riding around washouts, seeking directions, and grazing the horse made trips long. At night, travelers stopped at taverns for food and sleep. These had bad food, bad sleeping conditions, and no privacy.

Activity

Stage a debate between employer and employee during colonial times about limits on wages.

Name_____ Date_____

POINTS TO PONDER

1. Do you think the American attitude toward people who don't work has changed much since colonial times?

_____

_____

_____

_____

_____

2. For the person who was poor, was life better in America than in Europe? Why?

_____

_____

_____

_____

_____

_____

3. Today, we have minimum wage laws to protect workers from being underpaid. Why did the colonies have laws to prevent workers from being overpaid?

_____

_____

_____

_____

_____

Name_____ Date_____

CHALLENGES

1. If you saw a red or blue letter "P" on a person's shirt, what did the "P" stand for, and what kind of person was he?

_____

_____

2. What were two characteristics popular to Dutch homes?

_____

3. What style of building did the Swedes begin?

_____

_____

4. What were the basic farm tools of the colonial period?

_____

_____

5. Why didn't they put iron tips on their plows?

_____

_____

6. Why did frontier farmers prefer raising hogs over corn?

_____

7. What were the three main cash crops of the South?

_____

8. How many ships ran out of Boston in 1750?

_____

9. What was the purpose of the Navigation Acts?

_____

_____

10. Why wasn't a stop at a tavern always pleasant?

_____

_____

SOCIAL STATUS IN THE COLONIES

Where one ranks in one's community is very important to some people. Joining the right clubs, organizations, and teams in school may give a student social edge and prestige. Living in the wrong neighborhood may hurt one's status with other students. As important as it might be to modern Americans to be born into an important family, live in the right part of town, be seen with the right people, and attend the right school, it was much more important in colonial times.

The status of children was the same as their father's. Most children of the time were dressed in smaller versions of grown-up clothes and were expected to act like "little adults."

Americans adopted a RANKING SYSTEM from England and Europe where there were nobility (the royal family), the aristocracy (with titles like duke, earl, or lord), and commoners. At the bottom of European society were peasants. People were born into their status, and few rose above it.

Nobility did not move to the colonies, and titled aristocrats were few in number. America was a place where one could rise from the bottom to a position of importance and honor. At the top of American society were the better sort (large landholders, important merchants, and professionals: ministers, lawyers, and doctors). These were politely addressed as "Honorable," "Excellency," or at least: "Mr." or "Mrs." The middle class were the small landowners and shopkeepers who were addressed as "Goodman Smith" or "Goodwife Smith" or simply "Goody Smith." Unskilled workers who were free were called by their first name. Servants including indentureds, apprentices, free blacks, and slaves, were known only by their first name. Unlike England, status could change, and the released indentured servant might someday become "Goodman" and his son "Excellency."

Ranking went on all up and down the line. The most prominent planters looked down on those with smaller holdings in land and slaves. In Boston, it was said that the Cabots spoke only to the Lodges, and the Lodges spoke only to God. The minister with prominent church members had higher status than the one with only middle-class church members. Merchants were judged by the size of their store and quality of their customers. Even among slaves, there were ranks from household servants and skilled workers at the top to field hands at the bottom.

A WOMAN's status was determined by her husband's status. Legally, women were inferior; Blackstone's Commentaries said: "Husband and wife are one, and that one is the husband." Parents wanted their daughters to marry a man of distinction. In both England and the colonies, the wife was entitled to at least one-third of the property when her husband died, but American courts were willing to give her more if she was responsible for some of the husband's success. Before marrying again, widows often had prenuptial agreements drawn up to protect their inherited property for themselves and their children from previous marriages.

　　　　　　　　　30

A CHILD's status was that of the father, unless the mother was a slave, in which case the child was a slave even if the father was a free man. In schools, it was common for teachers to call the roll with the children of the most important families coming first.

SERVANTS formed the lowest class. Indentureds were those without enough money to pay for their ocean voyage. They signed a contract for free passage to America; that contract was sold to a farmer or merchant when they arrived, and they worked off the amount of passage. It often took five to seven years of hard work to pay for the trip. Convicts were also sent to relieve overcrowding in English prisons. They were often dangerous and unreliable workers; many ended up on American gallows. Apprentices were young people whose parents were either dead or too poor to support their children. Apprentices were to be trained by farmers or craftsmen so they could support themselves. New England colonies required that they be educated in reading, writing, and arithmetic.

The lives of white servants were usually miserable. Their masters wanted to get as much work with as little expense as they could from them. They were badly fed, poorly clothed, and abused by masters. If conditions got too bad, they often escaped to another colony.

Slaves. The first African-born "servants" arrived from the West Indies in 1619 and were apparently bound to an indenture of 20 years. After the time as servant ended, it is believed that they were freed. By 1675 they had become "servants for life" and then simply "slaves."

Before 1690 there were only 5,000 slaves in the 13 colonies. Few came directly from Africa. Most were born in the colonies or had been shipped to the mainland from the West Indies. A number of events occurred that increased the number of slaves: (1) The West Indies developed a surplus of slaves, so planters there sold off unneeded workers at a reasonable price in the 13 colonies; (2) Rice and tobacco growers needed many workers to produce the crop and could not find enough free laborers willing to work for low wages; (3) Slave codes were written making it clear that owners had complete control over slaves and could even kill them; and (4) It was too easy for indentureds and apprentices to escape, but blacks wandering free were easily identified in any crowd.

Slavery was practiced in all of the colonies; southern colonies had the most slaves, but New York had so many that one out of seven people in the colony was a slave. New England had only a few slaves, because farmers there had such small holdings that owning a slave was not very profitable. When the Revolution came, New Englanders were willing to give up slaves, but southerners still thought of slaves as useful laborers and refused to part with slavery. This was going to create serious problems later.

Activity

Make a list of people who might come into a colonial store, and put them in the order of their social rank.

Name_____ Date_____

POINTS TO PONDER

1. Do class distinctions still exist? In your town or city, what are the best neighborhoods or organizations that appeal to the elite?

_____

_____

_____

_____

_____

_____

2. Why do you think so few nobility or titled aristocrats moved to the 13 colonies?

_____

_____

_____

_____

3. Do you think that most of the servants worked any harder than they had to? Might that account for the frequent use of whips?

_____

_____

_____

_____

_____

_____

Name_____ Date_____

CHALLENGES

1. Which had higher rank, aristocracy or nobility? Why?

_____

_____

2. Give an example of the better sort who were probably not rich.

_____

_____

3. If you walked in a store, and the clerk addressed the woman as "Goody Jones," what could you assume about her?

_____

4. If he were talking to "Jim," what might you assume were possible positions Jim might hold?

_____

_____

5. Who was the most prominent Boston family?

_____

6. How long did it take for a person to work off an indenture?

_____

7. What group was trained by craftsmen in a trade?

_____

8. How many slaves were there in the 13 colonies in 1690?

_____

9. Which crops used the most slave labor?

_____

_____

10. Why didn't New England farmers use more slaves?

_____

_____

SLAVERY IN THE COLONIES

The London Company, which had established the Virginia colony at Jamestown in 1607, was dissatisfied with its slow growth. By the end of 1618 the colony had barely 1,000 settlers. To increase the labor force, the company sent 100 poor children as "bound apprentices" to the colony. The Virginians also found another source of workers. In August 1619 John Rolfe recorded the arrival of "a Dutch man of warre that sold us twenty Negars. [sic]" These and the small number of servants who followed were listed as "bound servants" and, like white servants, were apparently freed at the end of their service. One enterprising black, Anthony Johnson, came as a servant in 1622 but was himself an importer of white and black indentured servants by 1651.

By 1755 slavery was present in all of the English colonies in America.

Marylanders needed workers too, but they avoided using slave laborers because if the slaves converted to Christianity they might be freed. The Act of 1671 said a slave's religion did not affect his status, and more slaves were sold in the colony. South Carolinians had no qualms about using slaves but feared that so many would come that prices would fall. Georgia's founder, James Oglethorpe, intended that the colony's land should be reserved for English debtors; but when Georgians saw other colonies growing more wealthy, slavery came to their colony in 1755. Northern colonists preferred white indentured servants, and blacks were never more than two percent of their population.

Virginia had only 300 black servants in 1650. Three important changes occurred to increase the numbers of slaves in the colonies. First, the Company of Royal Adventurers was formed in 1663 and was to supply a minimum of 3,000 slaves annually to the American colonists. Second, the over-production of sugar in the West Indies resulted in soil depletion. As crops dropped and a demand for slaves increased on the mainland, West Indian planters sold off surplus workers to Americans. Third, a higher percentage of slave women came to North America than to the West Indies and Brazil. This increased the percentage of slaves who were American-born. Owners could see obvious possibilities of workers replacing workers through natural means, and they encouraged slave marriages.

To slaves, the friction between England and the American colonists must have produced some interesting discussions. Patrick Henry's famous statement, "Is life so sweet as to be purchased at the price of chains and slavery? . . . Give me liberty or give me death," may have seemed ironic. But the most curious statements of all belonged to slave-owning Thomas Jefferson. In his "Summary View," he said that the reason for the continued presence of the African slave trade was England's refusal to end it. In the Declaration of Independence, he penned the famous words: "All men are created equal" and among their inalienable rights were "life, liberty, and the pursuit of happiness." These words may have offered hope that things were about to change, but it was a false hope to those enslaved in the South, as they were soon to discover.

When the American Revolution started, some blacks were caught up in revolutionary fervor. At Breed's (Bunker) Hill, slaves and free blacks participated in the fighting. When Washington took command, he told recruiters not to enlist blacks, but some were already in the army. In October 1775 it was decided to bar blacks from the Continental Army. A month later, Governor Dunmore of Virginia declared that any black or indentured servant who joined the British army would be free. Slaves deserted the plantations and enlisted in the Royal army. Wherever the British army went, slaves flocked in. The seriousness of his mistake was made apparent to Washington when many of his own slaves escaped.

Wisely reversing policy, Washington ordered in December 1775 that free blacks might be enlisted in the Continental Army, and most states permitted both slave and free black enlistments in their militias. Massachusetts and Rhode Island had enough black volunteers to form separate regiments for them, but in many militia units black soldiers served with whites. New York allowed freedom to any slave serving for three years. Two states, Georgia and South Carolina, refused to enlist black troops; but even in those states, blacks were leaving plantations to serve on one side or the other. Black soldiers participated in every major battle from Breed's Hill to Yorktown.

By the time the U.S. Constitution was written, things had changed. The delegates that met at Philadelphia in 1787 faced many troubling issues. But no issue, including slavery, was worth running the risk of going home without a new, desperately needed constitution. The Confederation Congress had recently discussed slavery and had concluded in the Northwest Ordinance that slavery should not exist in territories north of the Ohio River. At the same time, Congress voted that any fugitive slave escaping to the region could be reclaimed by the master.

In Philadelphia, the Constitutional Convention could hardly dodge questions that slavery raised. Especially in regard to taxation without representation, feelings ran hot. The South feared that a poll tax might be levied and slaves would be counted as persons for taxation purposes. When representation was discussed, the North opposed counting slaves at all. A compromise was reached that for both taxation and representation, "all other persons" (slaves) would count as three-fifths of a person.

The North wanted to end the African slave trade. Most delegates from the upper South agreed, because they had all the slaves they needed. However, South Carolina and Georgia needed more slaves and wanted to import more. A compromise was reached allowing the trade to continue another 20 years.

There was almost no discussion on the question of whether fugitive slaves were to be returned if they crossed state lines. Article IV, Section 2, said that any person escaping labor or service in one state and fleeing to another, "shall be delivered up on claim of the party to whom such service or labor shall be due."

Activity

As a class, discuss the pros and cons of slavery from a colonial perspective. Don't forget that some state economies relied on slavery and also that slavery was not seen as purely "right" or "wrong" by every colonist.

Name_____ Date_____

POINTS TO PONDER

1. If you were a colonial farmer, would you prefer to use an indentured servant or a slave? Why?

_____

_____

_____

_____

_____

2. As a slave first listening to the Declaration of Independence being read, what thoughts might have gone through your mind?

_____

_____

_____

_____

_____

3. The writers of the Constitution never mentioned "slaves" or "slavery," but used terms such as "other persons," "persons held to service or labor," and "such persons." Why do you think they did this?

_____

_____

_____

_____

_____

Name_____ Date_____

CHALLENGES

1. What designation was given to the 20 Africans sold in 1619?

_____

2. Why were Marylanders concerned about slavery?

_____

_____

3. Why did Georgians start buying slaves?

_____

_____

4. What three changes occurred that brought more slaves into the colonies?

_____

_____

5. Why might slaves have hoped things would change after the Declaration of Independence was written?

_____

_____

6. What were the "inalienable rights" mentioned in the Declaration of Independence?

_____

7. According to the Declaration of Independence, who had these "inalienable rights"?

_____

8. Why did many blacks escape their plantations to fight in the British army?

_____

_____

9. Was there a question at the Constitutional Convention of ending slavery?

_____

10. Which states wanted to continue the slave trade? Why?

_____

_____

YOUNG PEOPLE'S LIVES IN THE COLONIES

For the young person today, life is made up of television, video games, sports, and of course, school. At home, there may be a few chores to do, but they aren't too time-consuming. There is generally enough room for each member of the family to get away to themselves once in a while. But what was it like for a young person in the 1600s and

Large families were the norm in colonial times. Children provided extra hands to help on the farm or in the family business.

1700s? Without the benefit of TVs, CDs, computers, or video games, how did they survive?

THE COLONIAL FAMILY. The colonial family was usually crowded into a small home. It was not uncommon to have 15 to 20 brothers and sisters. It was often true that of those brothers and sisters, many died at an early age. Many women died in childbirth; their husbands quickly remarried, so there were often many half-brothers and half-sisters as well.

By the time children were three or four years old, they had begun doing simple chores to help their father or mother. By the time they were 10, it was expected that they behave as adults. The laws regarding a child's behavior toward parents were severe in some colonies. In Connecticut, a never-enforced law provided the death penalty for any child or children above 16 years old who struck or cursed their parent, unless the parent had provoked them by extreme cruelty.

Girls were often married by the time they were 14 to 16, and parents worried about daughters not married by the time they were 20; if they weren't married by 25, they were almost hopeless and were sneeringly referred to as "spinsters." Young men usually married at 18 to 20 years old and moved away from the parents' home.

The American population was young; adults 60 to 70 years old were unusual, and anyone over 80 was almost unheard of. In cities, many young people lived on their own and needed social outlets. They joined fire brigades and militia units or formed young people's groups at churches. Literary societies gave an opportunity to meet a member of the opposite sex.

Since over 90 percent of Americans lived in rural areas, and the work was both hard and time-consuming, there was less chance for socializing than in cities. Young women found activities to do in groups: quilting bees, church socials, garden groups, and so on. Young men worked together in barn raisings, house raisings, militia, fox hunts, and so forth.

RECREATION. Children's play included marbles, tops, tag, pitching pennies, and games like "Button, Button." Girls enjoyed dolls; boys had toys. Hunting and fishing were practical but pleasurable activities for young men because they were fun and provided needed food. Game was abundant in most of the country, with turkeys, raccoons, weasels, beaver, and deer being common targets for the men. Fish were also in great supply and were easy to catch. Fishing rods, hooks, lines, and sinkers were imported from England. Trapping was another profitable activity.

Card playing was a very popular activity; one ship cargo included 1,584 decks of cards shipped to Boston. Heavy gambling in card games was common and led to some bankruptcies. Common people often gambled with dice and "huzzlecap" (pitching pennies).

Musical instruments were very popular in most colonies. These were played for individual pleasure and for concerts. Common instruments included the violin, flute, harpsichord, harmonica, guitar, and French horn. A few organs made it to the colonies and were mostly used in Anglican churches. Music was important to the people. Sailors were hired for sailing ships, with the captains considering their musical skills as well as seamanship. Thomas Jefferson, when building his home at Monticello, wanted workers who were not only good craftsmen, but also good musicians. Almost everyone, including slaves, played at least one instrument.

Singing was popular. In New England, singing masters went from town to town to hold singing schools. These were held during the winter and lasted two weeks. Everyone in town would come for three to four hours and sing hymns. Many pieces of secular (non-church) music were brought by the colonists from England. The most popular English ballads were "Barbara Allen" and "Greensleeves." A popular American song was "Springfield Mountain," about a boy who was bitten by a snake while mowing a field; his girlfriend, Molly, sipped the venom from his wound, and both died.

Dancing was popular among the people, with dances running from the dignified minuet to the jig, a dance popular among the slaves. Dancing schools opened in larger cities, and dignified balls were held on formal occasions. Mixed dancing (males touching females) was often criticized by ministers. Reverend Increase Mather wrote a 30-page attack on mixed dancing and warned parents that this activity clearly violated the seventh commandment ("Don't commit adultery"). He declared that parents did not know the moral damage they caused by allowing their children to dance; they were now properly informed.

Theater was slow in coming to the colonies, but it was popular everywhere except in Puritan and Quaker colonies by the time of the Revolution. Taverns and courtrooms were used as stages in the South before any theaters were built. The first theater built in the colonies was in Williamsburg, and many leading families, including the Washingtons and Jeffersons, attended performances there. Lewis Hallam and David Douglas, both English actors, formed traveling companies that toured the colonies in the 1750s and raised interest in theatrical performances. Shakespeare's plays were very popular as were a number of plays known today only by their titles.

Activity

Write a skit incorporating many of the facts you now know about the life of a young person in the colonial period.

Name_____ Date_____

POINTS TO PONDER

1. Why were farm families especially large in colonial times?

_____

_____

_____

_____

_____

_____

2. What were some colonial activities that still entertain young people?

_____

_____

_____

_____

_____

_____

3. How were young people's activities like and different from those of modern young people?

_____

_____

_____

_____

_____

_____

Name_____ Date_____

CHALLENGES

1. Why were there so many half-brothers and half-sisters in colonial families?

_____

_____

2. By what age did parents worry about whether their daughters were ever going to get married?

_____

3. What were some activities available in town for young men?

_____

_____

4. What were some activities in rural areas drawing girls together?

_____

_____

5. Why was hunting both pleasurable and practical?

_____

_____

6. What modern activity is the same as "huzzlecap"?

_____

7. What, besides seamanship, was an edge that might help a young man get hired on a ship?

_____

8. What was the most popular ballad written in America?

_____

9. Who was a critic of mixed dancing?

_____

10. What two English actors were most important in bringing theater to America?

_____

_____

COLONIAL CLOTHING

American colonial dress was very different in many ways from today's American clothing. Women in America made most of their families' clothes themselves. At first few ships traveled from Europe to the colonies, and supplies such as fabrics and dresses were not readily available. Cost was also a big factor, and colonists had little extra money to spend. Clothing was passed down from generation to generation. It was sometimes altered to suit the newest styles, but in colonial times styles varied little from year to year. Many times even

Styles from the late eighteenth century for the common folk (left) and the wealthy (right)

historians can't distinguish easily between the date of clothing in paintings from, for instance, 1600 and 1630! By the time the American Revolution began, styles were changing noticeably only over 10- to 15-year periods.

How did people know what the latest styles were? There were no magazines full of pictures of the latest fads in clothing. There were no sale bills advertising the newest fashions. In the 1600s, new styles developed through word of mouth. Colonists in coastal cities noted what newcomers from Europe were wearing. In the late 1700s some fashion plates began displaying the newest styles circulating among the more affluent people, but even these were not widely used until the 1800s. "Fashion babies," one-foot dolls wearing the newest styles, were also circulated in Europe and America about once a year in the late 1700s.

Colonial women made most of their clothing. Often, this meant not only sewing each outfit (by hand, since sewing machines hadn't been invented yet), but also growing the cotton, wool, or flax to spin into thread and yarn and then weaving this into fabric. This process took time and practice. One dress or suit might take months to make, so unless a colonist were wealthy, he or she would get a new outfit only on a very special occasion. A colonist who got one new outfit in a year in the 1600s was fairly well-off.

In both Europe and America until well after the American Revolution, children's clothing, both boys' and girls', was a replica of the mother's. Until they were about five years old, even the boys wore skirts. This made diaper changing easier. Little girls wore corsets and petticoats just like their mothers did. Their outfits certainly weren't very good play clothes, but children were brought up to be responsible, quiet, and hard-working. With chores and lessons often beginning at sunrise and ending after sunset, boys and girls from the age of five had little time for play anyway.

Men's clothing styles remained much the same throughout colonial times. Except for the wealthiest who could afford the frills of the English styles, most wore clothing in earth tones with very little decoration. Suit styles emphasized broad shoulders and narrow waists. Dress shirts were fitted and stiff, with a high collar. Work shirts were looser fitting. Men's breeches were tied just below the knee. Stockings covered the calves of their legs.

Women wore many layers of clothing. The chemise was a basic floor-length undergarment/nightgown. It usually had ruffled sleeves and a drawstring at the neck. Sleeve ruffles were often pulled down so they showed at the bottom of the dress sleeves for extra decoration. The neck of the chemise was also drawn up into view when lower necklines were worn, not only for decoration, but also for modesty.

Over the chemise at least two petticoats were worn. The under-petticoat was usually made of a plain fabric and wasn't dyed. The outer-petticoat was sometimes just as plain, but sometimes it was dyed either a solid color that would stand in contrast to the skirt, or it would be patterned in a contrasting stripe. Many times the outer-petticoats were heavily embroidered. Wealthy women might wear outer-petticoats made of satin or silk.

Between the petticoats, women wore either one or two pockets. Pockets were not sewn into skirts, but slits were left in skirts and outer-petticoats so that a lady could reach the pockets tied beneath. Ladies' pockets were quite large; since purses weren't carried until the 1800s, women put essentials in these pockets. Wealthier women might carry combs, head scratchers, fans, and smelling salts (they often passed out due to the tightness of their corsets and the heat from wearing all the clothes). These pockets were usually also embroidered, although they were never seen.

Corsets were an interesting aspect of women's clothes. In the 1600s, corsets were still made mainly of iron. By the 1700s they were being made of very stiff fabric that was made stiffer by metal or whale bone. At first these were made in two parts, called bodies, and laced or hooked up both the front and back. Eventually they were made into one piece. Often a dress bodice was also boned. Until the late 1700s, a stomacher was placed into the front of the bodice. This was a piece of wood, carved to fit the woman wearing it, that held the bulk of the skirts and petticoats flat.

The over-dress was made in at least two to five parts. The bodice mentioned above and an over-skirt were not sewn together and were always part of the dress. Sleeves tied on to the bodice instead of being sewn in (at times dress sleeves were not worn, but chemise sleeves still covered the arms). The bodice could be made in either two parts, as the corset was, or could be one piece, either lacing just up the front or just up the back.

The skirt of the over-dress was normally open down the entire front. Most ladies wore their over-dresses pinned up (most often with thorns) in such a way that their outer-petticoats could be seen. Some colonists thought this display of petticoats was sinful and left theirs closed.

Some religious sects wore darker shades of clothing. They believed that such things as curled hair, split skirts, and decorations such as embroidery and jewels were sinful. Many of these ladies wore white kerchiefs, aprons, and caps. Their influence was seen even in courtly American women, as all classes wore kerchiefs and aprons, in public as well as when they were working, even when they were obviously out of style in Europe.

Activity

Select a variety of pictures showing fashions from 1965 to 1995 as well as several prints from colonial America. Compare today's rapid changes to the slow changes of colonial America.

Name_____ Date_____

POINTS TO PONDER

1. People in colonial America received very little information about current trends in Europe. Any news that they obtained was months old, due to the time it took to travel across the ocean, as well as the time it took to spread the information once it arrived. How do you think this affected the colonists?

_____

_____

_____

_____

_____

2. Colonial Americans were very resourceful. If you were a designer in the early 1700s, how would you have attempted to make people on two continents aware of your newest fashions?

_____

_____

_____

_____

3. Some colonists were very much against trends such as low necklines, jewels, and revealed petticoats, yet their own children wore those styles as much as they could. What clothing in today's culture have you noticed one generation denouncing while another is applauding it? Why do you think this happens?

_____

_____

_____

_____

_____

Name_____ Date_____

CHALLENGES

1. Where did colonial families get most of their clothing? Why?

_____

_____

2. How fast did colonial styles change?

_____

3. How did colonists find out what the latest styles were?

_____

_____

4. What were fashion babies?

_____

_____

5. List the steps a colonial woman would take in making a dress.

_____

_____

6. How were young boys' clothes different in colonial times from what they are today?

_____

_____

7. How were colonial ladies' pockets different from today's pockets?

_____

8. What was the minimum number of pieces of clothing a colonial woman might wear in public?

_____

9. What was the maximum number of clothing pieces a colonial woman might wear?

_____

10. How did religion influence American clothing?

_____

_____

THE NEW MAN (AND WOMAN)

A Frenchman named Michel-Guillaume de Crévecouer came to the colonies in 1756 and changed his name and citizenship. He traveled through the colonies as a salesman, surveyor, and a keen observer. In 1769 he married and settled down as a farmer in New York. During this time, he wrote *Letters from an American Farmer.* From the beginning, he observed a big difference between Americans and Europeans. He asked the question: "What, then, is this American, this new man?" The American had come from Europe, and might be of English, Dutch, French, Swedish, or German ancestry, and yet he had changed his attitudes to become an independent thinker who took pride in hard work and his property. "The American is a new man, who acts upon new principles; he must therefore entertain new ideas, and form new opinions."

Michel-Guillaume de Crévecouer observed that even though settlers came from Europe, they became "new men" with new ideas when they became Americans.

Other observers who came later, especially Alexis de Tocqueville (who came in the 1830s) noticed this same thing. Americans were different. The questions were what made them different, and how did they differ from Europeans? Various explanations have been given, and some are included here. They are not listed in any order of preference.

THE ACT OF LEAVING. The European often lived in the same house with his parents and grandparents; perhaps the family had lived in the same town for the last 150 years. People did not leave roots this tightly held out of some whim. It was hard to say good-bye to nation, language, town, family, friends, and possessions to go down the road toward the coast. After boarding the ship, they suffered seasickness and watched as others suffered various diseases and died. After weeks at sea, land was sighted, and the passengers became excited. In their hearts, they knew this was now their homeland, and they would never return to the village of their youth or see their parents again.

Once in America, they did not regain the loyalty to one place that they had in Europe. They freely moved from one town and colony to another in pursuit of new opportunities. Crévecouer wrote that the European arriving in America had a limited idea of what he might achieve, but he quickly outgrew that. "Two hundred miles formerly appeared a very great distance, it is now but a trifle; he no sooner breathes our air than he forms schemes . . . he never would have thought of in his own country."

THE FEELING OF INDEPENDENCE. In Europe and England, the farmer often worked for a nobleman or landlord. The pay was low, and opportunities to ever own a sizable amount of land were almost impossible. In America, land was available, and many who started out poor were now wealthy landowners. With that came the realization that if a person fails, it is his own fault; he cannot blame it on the system. That meant hard work, but it also gave a purpose to that work. Owning land was important. Crévecouer wrote: "Happy those to whom this transition has served as a powerful spur to labour, to prosperity." Others were lazy, and their pride in ownership, he said, had led them to inactivity and wasteful efforts.

This independence allowed a person to try and fail; if he failed, he was free to try again. Americans did not look down on those who failed, only on those who made no effort to succeed. The American was free to try different occupations, to move to new lands, to rise in rank.

THE OPEN CLASS STRUCTURE. The idea of a self-made man (or woman) seems as American as apple pie. Not everyone climbed the ladder of success and achieved great things. However, every colony had its success stories of individuals moving up from the bottom to prominence. Indentureds became large landowners, apprentices became merchants, and sailors became shipowners. Any white could become a respected member of society. A classic example was William Phips who began as a frontiersman from Maine and rose to become royal governor of Massachusetts.

INFLUENCE OF THE FRONTIER. The frontier offered many immigrants their first step up the ladder of success. One did not have to be educated or come from a good background to be accepted. Ability with an ax and Pennsylvania rifle were enough to impress others, and qualities like courage, strength, and endurance could make a man a local hero.

UNDERRATED PEOPLE. The English and Europeans looked down on Americans. One English writer described Americans as a "mongrel breed of Irish, Scotch and Germans, unleavened with convicts and outcasts." All colonials were viewed as unwashed, uneducated, and uncivilized. This view totally ignored the resourcefulness of the frontiersman and the inquiring minds of a growing group of American thinkers and writers.

Books covering religion, medicine, science, history, political thought, and the classics (in the original Greek or Latin) were read by many American leaders. The more popular books of sermons contained more than just religion, they included common sense views of society. Readings in history often questioned the divine right of rulers (the idea that God appointed a person to rule, and anyone disagreeing with him was wrong and evil).

Almost without notice by Europe, America was producing poets such as Michael Wigglesworth and Anne Bradstreet, artists like John Copley and Benjamin West, physicians like Dr. Benjamin Rush, and scientists worthy of being accepted as members of the Royal Society (the top scientific group in England). If the colonies had produced no one else, they could have taken pride in the writings and experiments of Benjamin Franklin.

Activity

Put the reasons given for the differences between Americans and Europeans on a list, and ask students to put them in the order of their importance.

Name_____ Date_____

POINTS TO PONDER

1. What determines a person's success or failure in our time? Would colonial Americans have had the same views?

_____

_____

_____

_____

_____

2. Can a person today rise from the bottom to the top in America? What skills or training are important now that were not necessary in colonial times?

_____

_____

_____

_____

_____

3. Which of the reasons given seem most important in explaining the difference between the European and American? Why?

_____

_____

_____

_____

_____

_____

Name_____ Date_____

CHALLENGES

1. What book did Crévecouer write?

_____

2. What later writer also noticed a difference between Americans and Europeans?

_____

3. Why was the long ocean voyage important in separating colonists from their European past?

_____

_____

4. What was the disadvantage of failing in America?

_____

5. What was the American attitude toward failure?

_____

_____

6. Where did Sir William Phips begin, and where did he end?

_____

_____

7. What abilities impressed frontiersmen?

_____

_____

8. What was divine right?

_____

_____

9. Name two successful colonial American artists.

_____

10. What colonial Americans achieved greatness in literature and science?

_____

_____

THE HEAD UNDER THE CROWN

Suppose you work for a branch of a large company, and headquarters is thousands of miles away. You never see the president or vice presidents of the company. Do their decisions affect you? Certainly. In the same way, the 13 colonies were a branch office that seldom drew much attention at headquarters. But what went on in London had great effect on them. England's rulers often clashed with Parliament, and however the disputes ended, many on the losing side wanted to leave as soon as possible.

James I of England paid little attention to the colonies established in North America during his reign.

JAMES I was the first Stuart king of England. He was already Scotland's King James VI. Since he was Queen Elizabeth's cousin and closest living relative, he became king after her death in 1603. His fame today comes from the King James Bible, but in his own time, he was more noted for his belief in divine right (the doctrine that a king owes his crown to God, not the people). He spent money faster than it came in, doubling the national debt in four years. His support of the Anglican church caused the Puritans to leave. He paid little attention to North America. His interest was in Ireland, where he helped Protestants take land from Irish Catholics.

CHARLES I became king in 1625, clashed with Parliament almost immediately after he married a French Catholic princess who squandered a fortune, and punished Parliament leaders who dared oppose him. He abused power by creating a secret Court of the Star Chamber that punished people without a fair hearing. He ruled without a Parliament for 11 years but ran out of money and had to call a new Parliament in 1640. In 1642 civil war broke out between those loyal to the king (Cavaliers) and those backing Parliament (Roundheads). Parliament's army was led by Oliver Cromwell, a Puritan who wanted soldiers who did not swear or gamble and "trusted in God and kept their powder dry." After he was captured, Charles I refused to compromise with Parliament and was executed in 1649.

COMMONWEALTH. After beheading the king, Parliament declared that England was a republic, but the real power was with Cromwell's army, the "Ironsides." Many Cavaliers left, including the ancestors of George Washington, Thomas Jefferson, Patrick Henry, and Edmund Randolph. After quarreling with his first Parliament, Cromwell replaced them in 1653 with the "Little" Parliament with only 139 members. They named him "Lord Protector" (president) for life. Puritan rule was stern, and anything considered an amusement was stopped. Although he was Puritan, Cromwell helped the Quakers and allowed Jews to return to England. After Oliver Cromwell died in 1658, his son Richard tried to rule, but he was not up to the task and retired in 1659. For a time, England had no real government.

CHARLES II, son of Charles I, returned to England in 1660 and received a great welcome from the people. The Commonwealth was officially ended, but only a few of those involved in executing Charles I were punished; others fled to the colonies. The Anglican church was restored, and all ministers were required to use its prayer book. That led to the persecution of priests and ministers of all other churches. Charles II tried to rule without Parliament. When he ran short on cash, instead of calling Parliament together, he took a French bribe of £300,000, given on condition he make war on the Dutch. Charles secretly became Catholic just before he died in 1685.

JAMES II, brother of Charles II, replaced him. He had two goals: to rule without Parliament and to restore the Catholic Church. A revolt against the king was put down, and the judge who heard the cases against the accused made no pretense of justice in his court. By the time he was through, over 1,000 people had been flogged, sold into slavery, hanged, or beheaded. The king ordered seven bishops arrested for refusing to read a royal message giving Catholics more power. When a jury found the bishops not guilty, a great cheer went up throughout England. The final straw came when James' wife gave birth to a son who would be raised as a Catholic and be heir to the throne. Seven of England's leaders secretly invited Prince William of Orange to come to England with an army and put his wife Mary (who was a Protestant daughter of James II) on the throne. Landing with 14,000 men, William found the public overwhelmingly on his side; James tried to escape but was caught. William then let him escape to France.

WILLIAM AND MARY's reign offered an opportunity to make drastic changes. The Act of Toleration offered freedom of religion to all Protestants. The Bill of Rights (1689) made a number of changes: (1) The king could not keep an army without approval by Parliament; (2) Taxes had to be approved by Parliament; (3) Members of Parliament were to be elected without interference from the ruler; (4) Parliament should enjoy free debate; and (5) No Catholic or person married to a Catholic could rule England.

ANNE. Princess Anne, who came to the throne after William's death in 1702, was the younger sister of Queen Mary; one historian's view of her was that she was stupid, and her husband (Prince George of Denmark) was less intelligent than she. By the time of her death in 1714, all of her children were dead, so the throne went to a descendant of James I, a German named George, Elector of Hanover.

From 1607 to 1714, England went through dramatic changes in government that greatly affected the colonists. The struggles between king and Parliament were imitated in colonial conflicts between governors and legislatures. Each change in England brought a new group of settlers to the colonies. Americans saw the disadvantages of too much power in one person's hands, and more importantly, they saw the stupidity, greediness, and shortcomings of many of their British rulers.

Activity

Make a list of rulers from 1603 to 1714, and across from it list the religious groups that were in the most trouble during each king or queen's reign. Ask how this affected immigration to the colonies.

Name_____ Date_____

POINTS TO PONDER

1. Why might someone argue in favor of "divine right" and someone else oppose it?

_____

_____

_____

_____

_____

_____

2. What were some of the things the Stuart rulers did that caused one Stuart king to lose his head and another to lose his throne?

_____

_____

_____

_____

_____

3. Why was the struggle between king and Parliament important to American ideas later about the powers of the president and Congress?

_____

_____

_____

_____

_____

_____

Name_____ Date_____

CHALLENGES

1. Why was James I chosen as king?

_____

_____

2. What group left England because of his policies?

_____

3. Who were the Cavaliers? The Roundheads?

_____

_____

4. Who were some famous Americans whose relatives came to the colonies because of the outcome of the English Civil War?

_____

_____

5. Who ruled England during the Commonwealth?

_____

6. What group returned to England because of Cromwell's policies?

_____

7. What did Charles II do to avoid calling Parliament into session?

_____

_____

8. What was the relationship of William and Mary to James II?

_____

9. What church could a king or queen of England not belong to after the Bill of Rights was passed?

_____

10. What title did George I have before he became king?

_____

GOVERNMENT IN THE COLONIES

Imagine that the governor of your state was not elected by the people but was appointed by the president. The president inherited his job from his father and will be president until his death. The governor will be governor as long as he pleases the president. The governor almost always comes from outside your state, lives in a large mansion you have paid for, has total veto power, and any bill he refuses to sign can never become law. The upper house of your state

The capitol in Williamsburg, Virginia, where the House of Burgesses met

legislature is appointed by the governor. The lower house is mostly elected from the eastern part of your state, even though the western counties are growing rapidly. Your state judges are appointed by the governor from among the wealthy lawyers, landowners, and merchants. If you can picture this, you begin to understand how the colonies were governed.

Some felt this was the way government should be run, but others did not. Thomas Hobbes, an English writer, said that without government, people would destroy each other; governments were formed by the people to protect themselves, but once formed, they surrendered their freedom to their rulers. Hugo Grotius, a Dutch writer, said government was formed to protect rights and property; rulers existed for the benefit of the people, not the people for the benefit of rulers. John Locke believed that governments were formed to protect life, liberty, and property, but the individual had the right to either leave the country or resist any ruler who threatened those rights. Of all the writers, Locke's ideas had the greatest effect on the way Americans thought about government and their rulers.

COLONIAL GOVERNMENT. Every official was a substitute for someone in English government. The governor was a copy of the king; the legislature's upper house, the Council, imitated the House of Lords. The lower house was the American equivalent of the House of Commons. Colonial judges were more interested in pleasing the governor than the public.

GOVERNORS were appointed by the king in eight colonies, were selected by the proprietor in three colonies, and were elected in Connecticut and Rhode Island. If governors and legislators argued too much in proprietary and charter colonies, the king used it as an excuse to turn them into royal colonies, so both sides had good reason to work out differences quietly.

Royal governors were often distant relatives of the king or titled aristocrats who were not very wealthy and needed a job. Many were snobs who made no effort to appeal to the people they served. On the whole, they were not especially smart or honest. Bribe taking was common in England and Europe, and the favor of the governor could be had for a price. Governors often found ways to make money besides the salary paid by the colony.

Governors had many powers, among them, the power to veto bills passed by the legislature, to call the legislature into session and to send it home, to appoint judges and pardon offenders, to carry out laws, and to command military forces. His proclamations had the power of law.

COUNCILS were appointed by governors in royal colonies, were selected by proprietors in proprietary colonies, and were elected in charter colonies. "Councilors" were advisors to the governor and were sometimes the court of appeals. They were chosen from the most elite of the upper class. While it was an honor to be a councilor, they never had much independent power.

LOWER HOUSES went by various names: the House of Burgesses in Virginia, the General Court or Assembly in others. In early times, they were not very important, but as the House of Commons rose in power in England, lower houses grew in influence. Nearly all members of an assembly were chosen from among upper-class landowners, merchants, and leading lawyers. Many of those who led the states and Congress during the Revolution and Confederation had served in these lower houses.

COURTS. The colonists elected their justices of the peace, but they only tried minor cases. More important trials were presided over by judges chosen by the governor. In some colonies, the Council acted as the court of appeals. Beyond that, one might appeal to the Privy Council in London, but that was far too expensive for most colonists. When being tried, colonists were entitled to all the rights of an English citizen: trial by jury, the right to examine witnesses, and the right to be assumed innocent until proven guilty.

STRUGGLES BETWEEN GOVERNORS AND COLONISTS. The governor seemed to have all the power; he could not be fired and could veto any bill he chose. However, he had four major weaknesses. (1) His salary came from the legislature, so if he got too tyrannical, they could cut his pay or not pay him at all. (2) The legislature very carefully spelled out how money was to be spent to prevent the governor from using it as he wished. (3) Members of the legislature had connections in England. If they were too unhappy with the governor, they wrote to friends who pressured the king. If too much pressure built up, the king would recall the official. (4) Enough local pressure might be put on the governor to make him resign or, at least, suffer.

Governor William Cosby, New York's corrupt governor, was the target of articles in John Peter Zenger's *New York Journal.* Cosby took Zenger to court on a charge of seditious libel (treasonable lies). Zenger's lawyers were able to prove that what was written was true, and the jury found Zenger not guilty. The governor was humiliated. He died a year later.

Some quarrels turned violent. That was the case during Bacon's Rebellion in Virginia. Bacon feuded with Governor Berkeley, which led to the governor charging him with being a rebel. Bacon attacked Jamestown and then burnt the capital, and Berkeley raised an army to crush the rebels.

Activity

Have the students make a list of the way colonial governments were different from modern state governments.

Name_____ Date_____

POINTS TO PONDER

1. If you were the ruler, how would you like the colonial system? Why?

_____

_____

_____

_____

2. Councils were often called "rubber stamps" for the governor. Would you agree with that view? Why or why not?

_____

_____

_____

_____

_____

3. Of the four methods of controlling a royal governor, which two seem to be the best ways of keeping him under control?

_____

_____

_____

_____

_____

Name_____ Date_____

CHALLENGES

1. Which writer believed the citizen must always obey the law?

_____

2. Which writer believed that if the government started taking away life, liberty, and property, a citizen had the right to rebel?

_____

3. What was the colonial equivalent of the House of Lords?

_____

4. What two colonies elected their governors?

_____

5. Did royal governors have to please the people? Why?

_____

_____

6. Why did proprietary governors and legislatures work well together?

_____

_____

7. Who made up the lower houses?

_____

_____

8. Who acted as the court of appeals in most colonies?

_____

9. How could the legislature discourage the governor from vetoing its bills?

_____

_____

10. What journalist was found not guilty in a libel case?

_____

NEW FRANCE

To the north of the 13 British colonies lay the colony of New France. Founded in 1608 by Samuel de Champlain, it covered the enormous area from the St. Lawrence River valley northward. Even though it had far fewer settlers than the 13 colonies, it was not going to be easy to capture.

GOVERNMENT. The system used in New France was much different from that used in English colonies. In the 13 colonies, bills passed by the legislature and approved by the governor went to the Privy Council (the king's advisors) for final review; if they opposed the bill, it was not law. The system began with colonists and moved up.

In New France, by contrast, law moved from the top down. The <u>King of France</u> had the power to make new laws; after his laws were

Samuel de Champlain founded the French colony of New France.

sent to the Sovereign Council of New France, they immediately went into operation.

The <u>Sovereign Council</u> was made up of the governor, bishop, and five appointed councilors (later increased to 12). The Council made laws on a subject until the King's regulations arrived; it was also the supreme court for the colony. An official who, in fact, had more power than the governor was the <u>intendant.</u> He was responsible for carrying out the king's policies. He was in charge of the courts, police, taxation, and spending of colony funds. In each community, the militia captain was responsible to him. The captain saw that the laws and intendant's policies were obeyed. Intendants, as heads of the legal system, punished criminals and settled disputes between colonists.

The system was not smooth, and lines of authority were often questioned. Governors and intendants were usually furious with each other. The Catholic church was a very important part of colonial government as well, and the bishops refused to give up spiritual leadership. When Bishop Laval arrived in New France, he was deeply concerned about the corruption of the natives by liquor. He warned traders not to sell or give brandy to the natives. If they violated his order, they were to be excommunicated (removed from membership in the church). Those in the government wanting to increase the fur trade protested Laval's policy.

Catholic missionaries worked among the Hurons and other Algonquian tribes to convert them. After a long struggle with the Iroquois, many Hurons were captured by their enemies, and both Hurons and priests were tortured and killed. Governor Frontenac strengthened defenses at white settlements, but after he was dismissed in 1689, Iroquois attacked the village of Lachine, killed 85 residents, and took 100 captives away to be tortured to death later. Frontenac was sent back to take charge again.

ECONOMIC LIFE. In 1627 the <u>Company of One Hundred Associates</u> was set up and given all the land from Florida to the North Pole. Its purpose was to settle the region and bring the natives "to the knowledge of the true God." Each member was given a large grant of land. The company hoped to bring French peasants to work the land for the land owners.

The company had little success in persuading peasants to leave their homes in sunny France to live in the colder climate of New France, where their lives might be shortened by the Iroquois. Officers who served in New France were offered grants of land if they stayed. Frenchmen were offered free passage and land on reasonable terms. Women between 16 and 40 who were strong and healthy were sent. Orphans were a good source of settlers. To increase the number of inhabitants, a law was issued in 1669 punishing the parents of unmarried children whose daughters had reached the age of 16 and whose sons had reached the age of 20 without either marrying or becoming priests or nuns. Couples with ten living children were given 300 livres a year, and for 12 children parents received 400 livres a year.

Landholders hoped that workers would be content to work their land on the same terms that French peasants received. Of those who went, many were tempted to go out into the forests and trade furs illegally. These were called *coureurs de bois* (outlaws of the bush). Francis Parkman described the coureur as a "strange figure, sometimes brutally savage, but often marked with lines of daredevil courage, and a restless, thoughtless gayety [sic]." He was a person who "liked the woods because they emancipated him from restraint." Coureurs were not popular with the church because of their wild ways and their corruption of the morals of the natives; landlords did not like them because they did little work and tempted workers to escape their responsibilities. Bernard DeVoto said English and Scottish fur traders found them "dirty, profane, excitable, noisy, forever talking, forever singing, comradely with Indians who were even grimier than they."

Compared with the 13 English colonies, New France was very weak and could easily be taken in a war. The first census was taken in 1666, and it reported the total population was 3,215. By 1698, it was up to 15,255. All of its European population was in a thin line along the St. Lawrence River. If war occurred and the English captured any major point along the river, they could cut off all settlements west of there. New France had a very small population. In 1698 Quebec was a city of 1,900; Montreal had 1,300; and 200 lived at Trois-Riviéres.

To protect the colony, the French worked hard at building forts, training militia, and building friendships with the natives. Despite the fact that English settlers out-numbered them 20–1, the French were more unified and prepared for a war in the forests than were the English.

Activity

A meeting takes place in your classroom with a Huron, a coureur, the bishop, a fur merchant, and an army official present. The subject is: "How does the fur trade affect the defense and prosperity of the colony?"

Name_____ Date_____

POINTS TO PONDER

1. Why were governors of New France happiest when there were no intendants appointed for the colony?

_____

_____

_____

_____

_____

2. Trade with the natives was a difficult problem. Why would a priest and fur merchant look at it differently?

_____

_____

_____

_____

_____

3. The French wanted to bring a feudal system to North America. Why was that idea doomed from the beginning?

_____

_____

_____

_____

_____

Name_____ Date_____

CHALLENGES

1. Who had the power to make any law he wished for New France?

_____

2. What were two duties of the Sovereign Council?

_____

_____

3. Who was responsible for seeing that the king's wishes were carried out in New France?

_____

4. What business did Bishop Laval try to stop?

_____

5. What happened to many priests working with the Huron?

_____

_____

6. What organization was formed to settle New France?

_____

7. By what ages were a young woman and young man required to be married to avoid having their parents punished?

_____

8. What was the reward for a couple producing 12 living children?

_____

_____

9. Why weren't coureurs popular with the church?

_____

_____

10. What was the combined population of Quebec and Montreal in 1698?

_____

_____

WARS COME TO NORTH AMERICA

New France and the 13 British colonies were like tails on dogs: wherever the dog (mother country) went, they (the colonies) were taken along behind. Four wars were fought between England and France from 1689 to 1763. These wars may seem small to us, but they were big to those who lived along the frontier and were in danger of attack by scalping parties.

KING WILLIAM'S WAR (1689–97) began when King William opposed King Louis XIV's desire to expand French territory in Europe. The 70-year-old governor, Count Frontenac, built up New France's defenses and inspired the Indians to join the French by leading them in a war dance. He wanted to attack New York, but gave up his plan when France did not send the needed

Lord William Pitt, the English prime minister, put great emphasis on the war in North America and sent skilled generals to fight the French and their Indian allies.

troops. An expedition by New England colonists captured Port Royal (on the west side of Acadia) in 1690. Sir William Phips attacked Quebec with 31 ships, but they were repulsed.

The war reached Schenectady, New York, where two guards had decided that instead of standing in the cold, they would build snowmen and dress them to look like guards. The attackers were not fooled, and they killed 60 settlers and took 27 captives away. At Haverhill, Massachusetts, a small Indian raiding party had the misfortune of capturing Hannah Dustin. After they killed her baby and taunted her, she killed and scalped ten of her captors during the night. The peace treaty restored the status quo, and nearly all property was returned to its former owners.

QUEEN ANNE'S WAR (1702–13) began with a dispute over who should rule Spain. By the time it was over, the English succeeded in taking most of Florida, and a French-Indian force destroyed Wells, Maine, and Deerfield, Massachusetts, where they killed 50 and took 111 prisoners. A British-New England force captured Port Royal again. The peace treaty gave Acadia and Newfoundland to England. After the war, France began building outposts in the Mississippi valley, including New Orleans (Louisiana) and Fort De Chartres (Illinois). They gained control of Lake Champlain by building Crown Point.

KING GEORGE'S WAR (1744–48) featured the usual border attacks on New York and New England. The most notable event of the war was the capture of Louisbourg (on Cape Breton Island). With its high, stone walls and a professional army garrison, the French laughed when the untrained New Englanders threatened their "Gibralter of America." Nevertheless, the colonists overran one of the outer walls and used the captured guns to blast the fort. In 49 days, the French surrendered. The peace treaty returned Louisbourg to France, but the experience of having captured it from professional soldiers added to colonial confidence.

FRENCH AND INDIAN WAR (1754–63) Everyone knew the treaty ending King George's War did not end the feud between England and France. As soon as the ink was dry on the treaty, both sides started preparing for the next war. The French started building forts along the Ohio River, on land claimed by Virginia. Virginia Governor Robert Dinwiddie sent 21-year-old George Washington to inform the French they were trespassing on Virginia soil. The French made it clear to Washington they intended to stay. Dinwiddie then sent Washington with 150 men to build a fort at the point where the Ohio River forms. On their way, scouts told Washington the French were already building a fort there (Fort Duquesne). Washington's men were spotted by a French scouting party at Great Meadows. Advance or retreat were both risky, so he ordered his men to build an earthworks he called "Fort Necessity." When a large French force arrived, the Virginians surrendered.

General Edward Braddock arrived in the colonies in 1755 with British regulars. He divided his men into four groups and took a group with him to attack Fort Duquesne. Colonel Washington, with 450 Virginia militia, accompanied the expedition. They were met by a smaller French force in an open field. After the first French volley, Braddock's army broke, and Washington's militia covered the retreat. The Indians quickly lined up behind the French. Maryland and Virginia rushed to build blockhouses at the mountain passes. In 1756 France and England were officially at war; Americans call it the French and Indian War, and Europeans call it the Seven Years' War.

The British war effort stumbled along until Lord William Pitt became prime minister. Pitt put great emphasis on the war in North America and sent some of his best generals to fight it. General John Forbes was to capture Fort Duquesne, but the French abandoned and destroyed the fort before his army reached it. General James Abercromby attacked the new French fort at Ticonderoga with 15,000 troops, but French General Montcalm's defenses and 3,600 men stopped them. Generals Jeffrey Amherst and James Wolfe succeeded in capturing Louisbourg. The most decisive battle of the war was fought outside Quebec on the Plains of Abraham in 1759. There, the British defeated the French in a struggle that killed both Wolfe and Montcalm.

That ended the war in North America, although it continued in Europe, the West Indies, and Asia for another three years. In 1763 the Treaty of Paris gave England all French territory east of the Mississippi except New Orleans and two islands in the St. Lawrence Bay. Spain gave up Florida to England but received the French territory west of the Mississippi River (Louisiana). Americans saw great opportunities to expand now that France was no longer in the picture. The English left the war with a large national debt. The French had been humiliated and looked for ways to get revenge.

Activity

Look on a historical map to see what would have happened if the French had won at Fort Duquesne and Quebec. What kind of peace treaty would France have forced on England?

Name_____ Date_____

POINTS TO PONDER

1. If you had been a frontiersman, what would you have thought when you learned that another war had started between England and France?

_____

_____

_____

_____

2. If you were George Washington, what would you have thought about the British regulars after Braddock's defeat?

_____

_____

_____

_____

_____

3. What did the peace treaty do to French influence in North America?

_____

_____

_____

_____

Name_____ Date_____

CHALLENGES

1. How did Frontenac win the Indians over to the French side?

_____

_____

2. How did Hannah Dustin get revenge?

_____

_____

3. What happened to Deerfield, Massachusetts, during Queen Anne's War?

_____

_____

4. What important outpost did France build at the mouth of the Mississippi River after Queen Anne's War?

_____

5. Why did New Englanders feel good about capturing Louisbourg, even after it was returned to France?

_____

_____

6. Why was Washington first sent to the Ohio valley in 1754?

_____

_____

7. What did Washington name his fort on the Great Meadows?

_____

8. Who in British government decided to emphasize the war in North America?

_____

9. Who captured what remained of Fort Duquesne?

_____

10. What two generals were killed at the Battle of Quebec?

_____

BEGINNINGS OF CONFLICT (1763–1766)

The French and Indian War had been a learning experience for colonists who fought in the war. The British had looked down on them; Wolfe called them "contemptible cowardly dogs." The colonials did not care much for the redcoats either: they considered them too immoral and led by brutal officers.

In 1763 colonists heard the joyous news: "France ousted from North America." The natives would no longer be stirred up by the French, more settlers would come, and the frontier could move beyond the mountains. The 200 blockhouses, built at mountain passes to stop

Rioters protesting the Stamp Act and other taxes hung tax collectors in effigy.

Indian attacks, could now be torn down. Then, just as the war was winding down, Pontiac, an Ottawa chief, stirred up tribes north of the Ohio River. He planned to destroy every British post west of the mountains. Many smaller forts were seized by the Indians, but Detroit and Fort Pitt held. These defeats hurt Pontiac's plans, but even worse for him was France's defeat in the war.

To satisfy English fur merchants and reduce the chance of another Indian uprising, the PROCLAMATION OF 1763 was passed by Parliament. No one could settle beyond the crest of the Appalachian Mountains. To enforce the law, 6,000 British troops were sent to North America. Frontiersmen were upset by the Proclamation Line, but most colonists did not care.

The years of war had been costly to England. Despite heavy taxes, the national debt stood at £129.5 million in 1764, far too high to suit Parliament. They chose George Grenville to solve the problem. Grenville was the right man for the job. Tight-fisted and hard-headed, he intended to raise money not only in England, but in the colonies as well. It was his financial policy, not the Proclamation Line, that aroused their fury.

England had always claimed the right to control its colonists. The king's Board of Trade never wanted them to compete against British industries. From the beginning, the British believed colonies existed for the good of the mother country, to supply it with raw materials and buy its products. The NAVIGATION ACTS (passed from 1650–1767) were part of that policy. The acts limited what could be shipped and who could ship it. To enforce these acts, the "writ of assistance" was created in 1696. It allowed customs collectors to search anywhere for smuggled goods. The Navigation Acts were seldom enforced, however, and were ignored by colonists.

Now England needed to raise more tax money, and it seemed to Grenville that since Americans had gained the most from victory over France, they should be willing to pay some of the cost. The SUGAR ACT (1764) reduced the tax on sugar from the old six pence to three pence per gallon, but this time, Grenville intended to see that the law was enforced. Customs laws were tightened; anyone accused of smuggling was presumed guilty and had to prove his innocence in Admiralty court, not before a jury.

The CURRENCY ACT (1765) said colonies could not issue paper money. This hurt colonies short on currency and seemed to colonists to be an attempt to ruin their economies. Merchants in Boston and New York protested by refusing to buy some British products.

The QUARTERING ACT (1765) required colonies to supply housing and supplies for British troops. That same year, the STAMP ACT was passed. It required people to purchase a revenue stamp for every newspaper, legal document, insurance policy, deck of cards, and die. Americans argued Parliament had no right to levy a direct tax on Americans who were not represented in Parliament. Others said it hurt the already weak economy.

Two colonists were especially important in protesting the new policies. James Otis was a brilliant, hot-headed Boston lawyer who saw the threat of using the writs of assistance as a weapon by royal officials to harass colonists. He charged it violated the sacred principle that "a man's home is his castle." In Virginia, Patrick Henry blasted the British policy of taxation without representation (taxing people not represented in Parliament) and advised George III to remember what had happened to Julius Caesar and Charles I. In Parliament, Colonel Issac Barré, an admirer of Americans, called them "Sons of Liberty."

Sons of Liberty organizations developed in northern cities during the summer of 1765. Their purposes were to force stamp agents to resign and "persuade" merchants to cancel orders for British goods. Their riots and looting of homes of royal officials caused all stamp agents to resign before the Stamp Act ever went into effect.

The STAMP ACT CONGRESS met in New York in June 1765 and was attended by delegates from nine colonies. After expressing their loyalty to the king, they denied that his government had the right to tax without consent of the governed; only colonial legislatures could tax Americans, they said. More important than resolutions were agreements by merchants not to purchase English goods until the Stamp Act was repealed.

In Parliament William Pitt spoke up for the Americans and called for the repeal of the Stamp Act. Spokesmen from the colonies were allowed to speak on the floor of the House of Commons. Benjamin Franklin spoke for Pennsylvania and told the members how expensive the war had been for his colony and how the Stamp Act would ruin the colonial economy. Repeal of the bill was supported by King George III as well, and it passed. The same day, however, Parliament passed the DECLARATORY ACT, claiming they had every right to pass any kind of law they chose to regulate the colonies.

Americans cheered repeal of the Stamp Act and totally ignored the Declaratory Act. In New York, statues were erected honoring Pitt and the king. The crisis seemed to have passed; in fact, it was only beginning.

Activity

Make a list of Americans who were going to be hurt by British policies from 1763 to 1765. Were people more interested in their billfolds or their rights?

67

Name_____ Date_____
POINTS TO PONDER

1. Why were frontiersmen more upset by the Proclamation Line than settlers along the coast were?

_____

_____

_____

_____

_____

_____

2. What is a boycott? Why is it effective?

_____

_____

_____

_____

_____

_____

3. Some people had suggested that the colonists be given a few seats in Parliament (perhaps as many as 20 or 30). Was that what they were wanting when they protested the Stamp Act?

_____

_____

_____

_____

_____

_____

Name_____ Date_____

CHALLENGES

1. At what points on the frontier did Pontiac fail to achieve his goals?

_____

_____

2. Why did Parliament create the Proclamation Line?

_____

_____

3. Where did Grenville intend to raise the money England needed?

_____

4. What had the Navigation Acts been created to do?

_____

_____

5. What was a writ of assistance? Can you think of a modern document that resembles a writ of assistance?

_____

6. Where was a person accused of smuggling sugar to be tried?

_____

7. What did merchants do to protest the Currency Act?

_____

_____

8. Why did Americans say Parliament could not require them to pay the Stamp tax?

_____

_____

9. Who were two of the most outspoken critics of the Stamp Act?

_____

10. What did the Declaratory Act say?

_____

_____

NEW TAXES AND A MASSACRE (1767–1770)

The Stamp Act crisis had passed, and traditional loyalties had not been strained at all among most American colonists. Even the Proclamation Line was not the big problem frontiersmen expected; as tribes gave up land in treaties, western regions opened to settlers. Loyalty to England remained strong, but new trouble was brewing.

Opponents of the Stamp Act were not all satisfied with passing polite resolutions. The Sons of Liberty were not great thinkers but men who enjoyed an

Paul Revere's engraving of the Boston Massacre helped stir anti-British sentiment in the colonies.

occasional riot. In 1766 the Sons of Liberty in New York erected a "liberty pole." When British soldiers tried to destroy it, colonists gathered to protest. A leader of the Sons of Liberty was injured in the scuffle that followed. Another incident occurred after the New York legislature was told it must pay part of the cost of British troops stationed in the colony, and it refused. In 1767 the legislature gave in to intense pressure and appropriated £3,000 to pay for the troops.

Pitt returned as prime minister in 1767, but his health was poor, so the real power was in the hands of Charles Townsend, Chancellor of the Exchequer (equivalent to our Secretary of Treasury). Townsend's heavy drinking had earned him the name of "Champagne Charley," but he was clever. If Americans did not like taxes paid directly for the upkeep of British troops, they might accept indirect taxes paid for certain products shipped from England. Since colonists were required to buy all of certain goods from England, those would be included on a new list for taxing: glass, paint, lead, paper, and tea. These TOWNSEND ACTS were expressly for the purpose of providing money for the defense and government of the colonies.

As might be expected, the colonists were not pleased. They did not want to give up any of their income to finance English control of the colonies. In 1768 the Massachusetts House sent the CIRCULAR LETTER to other colonial legislatures. It charged that Parliament had violated a "sacred" principle of English rights by these taxes: "that what a man has honestly acquired is absolutely his own, which he may freely give, but cannot be taken from him without his consent." Nor were they interested in sending delegates to Parliament; there would be too few and the cost too high to even consider it.

Many colonists decided to boycott British goods. Boston merchants agreed to stop importing British goods if merchants in other cities would cooperate. Other New England towns and New York's businessmen agreed. Philadelphia merchants were slow to follow.

Meanwhile, Royal customs officials were finding it hard to enforce the Townsend Acts, as no one voluntarily permitted them to search their property. Boston's customs officers felt they needed support from the Royal Navy, and the 50-gun frigate *Romney* was sent down from Halifax. With its guns behind them, officials could deal with the case of John

Hancock's ship, *Liberty.* When it had arrived in Boston harbor in May 1768, its captain had reported to the inspector, Thomas Kirk, that its cargo was only 25 casks of wine. Kirk said he was shoved into a cabin, held there while the ship was unloaded, and advised to keep his mouth shut or else. A crew from the *Romney* was sent to seize the *Liberty,* which was sailed from the wharf and anchored next to the *Romney.*

Bostonians did not like the *Romney,* its captain, crew, or reason for being there. An angry crowd attacked the customs officials still on the dock and that evening, threatened their homes. The next day, the customs collectors retreated to the safety of Castle William on an island in the harbor. The governor secretly urged General Gage to come with an army to Boston.

After Governor Bernard ordered the legislature to rescind (take back) the Circular Letter in September 1768, it refused to do so by a 92–17 vote. The number "92" became a symbol of resistance. Rumors spread that four regiments of redcoats were being sent to Boston, stories the governor refused to admit or deny. Gage and two regiments of redcoats arrived in October and encamped in front of John Adams' home.

Adams was a rising young attorney who had recently been asked to be a lawyer for the royal governor and had refused. Now he appeared in court as an attorney for Hancock's defense in the *Liberty* case. Since there was no proof Hancock knew what was on board the ship, Adams asked, how could he be held responsible? Besides, the punishment was too great for the crime. The case lingered for months before the government finally withdrew it.

The Circular Letter had its desired effect. In May 1769, Virginia voted its support for the Massachusetts position. A boycott of British goods spread over all the colonies. And most important, Governor Bernard sailed away from the colony, leaving Lieutenant Governor Thomas Hutchinson in charge.

In 1770 tension ran high in Boston. A boy had been killed in February by a British informer. The funeral procession included 500 children following the casket, along with many adults. A few days later, a brawl took place between some soldiers and civilians, but no one was killed.

On March 5, a lone sentry was on duty outside the customs house when a mob gathered around him and threw snowballs and stones at him. He called for help, and his sergeant came with seven men; soon, Captain Thomas Preston arrived. After one soldier was knocked down, another fired his musket, and then the rest fired theirs. Three civilians, including Crispus Attucks, were killed, and eight were wounded. The soldiers had a hard time finding lawyers to defend them, but Josiah Quincy and John Adams took the unpopular jobs. No one could prove the captain had ordered anyone to fire, so he was freed. Adams showed that the enlisted men were provoked beyond human endurance, and the jury found all but two not guilty. Those two were given the minimum punishment for manslaughter: branding on their thumbs.

Activity

Many things are happening in the colonies from 1767 to 1770. Some colonists are saying that it's time to leave the British empire; others still want to be loyal. Stage a debate between speakers on both sides of the question.

Name_____ Date_____

POINTS TO PONDER

1. A common phrase used today is: "They just don't get it." How might it have been applied to Townsend?

_____

_____

_____

_____

_____

2. If you had sat on the jury in the *Liberty* case, would you have voted for the defense or prosecution? Why?

_____

_____

_____

_____

_____

3. Do you think the British soldiers involved in the "Boston Massacre" were guilty of manslaughter?

_____

_____

_____

_____

_____

Name_____ Date_____

CHALLENGES

1. What caused the New York riot in 1766?

_____

_____

2. What is the job of Chancellor of the Exchequer similar to?

_____

3. What kind of taxes did Townsend think Americans might accept?

_____

4. What were four items Townsend chose to tax?

_____

_____

5. What did Massachusetts find was wrong with the idea of sending delegates to Parliament?

_____

_____

6. Why was the *Romney* sent to Boston?

_____

_____

7. Who owned the *Liberty?*

_____

8. What did the number "92" come to stand for?

_____

9. What happened in the *Liberty* case?

_____

_____

10. What lawyer was involved both in defending Hancock and the British soldiers involved in the "Boston Massacre"?

_____

GEORGE III & COMPANY

Since 1689 the power of England's rulers had been limited. The Bill of Rights had included such provisions as: (1) the king could not keep a standing army in peacetime without Parliament's consent, (2) no money could be taken from the treasury without Parliament's consent, (3) the king could not interfere with the election of members of Parliament, and (4) the king was not to interfere in any way with the enforcement of laws. These limitations on royal power were not challenged by William and Mary. Queen Anne had ideas about divine right, but never challenged Parliament's power to rule. It was not until the third ruler of the House of Hanover came to the throne that problems arose.

George III, unlike his predecessors, took an active role in government. He was especially annoyed with the American colonists.

In history, as in life, the personalities of people create the situations that develop. A calm and steady person can find room to compromise, but one with an ax to grind will turn a molehill into a mountain. In the 1770s, on both sides of the Atlantic, individuals existed who took small events and turned them into crises. This section deals with British leaders of that time who found ways to antagonize the Americans into revolting.

To understand GEORGE III (1738–1820) something needs to be known about his family. His great-great-grandfather was George I (1660–1727). A very difficult man to like, he threw his wife in prison for adultery while he was having affairs with two women. He was Elector (ruler) of Hanover, a small German state, when he was chosen to be king of England (because he was related to James I). He knew no English and communicated with his prime minister in Latin. When bills were passed by Parliament, he signed them without understanding or caring what they were about. During his reign, Parliament was free to do whatever it liked.

George II (1683–1760) was hated by both his parents, and both of them wished he was dead. He disappointed them by living. To control George II, his prime ministers talked with the queen, who then advised the king. His knowledge of English was poor, and he had the bad habit of throwing his wig at those who disagreed with him. He hated his son, Frederick, and ordered him to stay away from the palace. Frederick died before George II, but Frederick's son became George III.

George III was 22 years old when he became king in 1760. As a young ruler, he was under his mother's influence. She told him to "be King." Unlike the first two Hanovers, he wanted to be involved in government. He helped friends get elected to Parliament and worked to defeat enemies. His relations with Pitt, Grenville, and Townsend were often strained, but in Lord North, he found a leader who obeyed his wishes. He inherited his family's hot temper and was very annoyed by the Americans. In 1774 he said: "Blows must decide whether they are to be my subjects or independent." He intended to show them who was boss.

74

Unlike the Hanovers before him, George III was a faithful husband and a good father to his 15 children. A man of simple tastes, his favorite supper was boiled mutton and turnips. He liked to garden and build model ships.

LORD NORTH (1732–92) was the king's chief advisor. Although he refused to be called "prime minister," he ran the House of Commons for the king. A clumsy, awkward man with thick lips and a wide mouth, his eyes rolled constantly. He understood better than most the issues that troubled American colonists, but when the king wanted them punished, he obeyed. North wanted to resign many times, but the king would not let him, so he stayed. In 1782 he finally quit over the king's objections.

It was Lord North's responsibility to find military leaders to take charge of the war with the colonists. The best general in the army (Jeffrey Amherst) and the best admiral in the navy (Augustus Keppel) turned down the assignment, as did seven others, before William Howe accepted.

GEORGE GERMAIN (1716–85) was the Secretary of State for War and for the Colonies. During the Revolution, it was his responsibility to develop a winning strategy. Germain's family was prominent, and he entered the army as a captain, rising to the rank of major general. At the Battle of Minden in 1759, he repeatedly refused orders to advance. He was court-martialed. The officers found him guilty and "unfit to serve his majesty in any military capacity whatever." George II ordered that the sentence be read to British troops around the globe to convince them that being born to a high status was no shelter for the cowardly.

Germain had since risen in influence again and was a close friend of Lord North in Parliament. As a military expert, he issued detailed orders to his officers in America, but they ignored his orders, pointing out that the situation had changed during the weeks between letters. In the backs of their minds, the generals in America probably remembered well the court-martial in 1759 and felt that Germain was unworthy to tell them what to do.

THE EARL OF SANDWICH (1718–92), the First Lord of the Admiralty, was noted for his corruption: gambling, bribe taking, and waste of naval funds. It was his habit of eating his meat between pieces of bread that made him famous, not his ability to properly run a fleet. Supplies were stolen, positions were bought, and unseaworthy ships went to sea. The king believed the navy was strong, because Sandwich told him so. The king was the only one who trusted him. Many in the navy almost hoped for defeat so the Admiralty would be fired. Admiral Barrington described the Admiralty as the "wickedest herd that ever good men served under."

Historian Barbara Tuchman has stated that the main fault of Germain and Sandwich was that neither had a clear plan of strategy and that both were sloppy about the way they carried out the plans they tried.

Activity

List the weaknesses you saw in the king and his chief advisors. As a colonist, ask what the class impression is of His Majesty and his government's leaders.

Name_____ Date_____

POINTS TO PONDER

1. What characteristics did George III have that were different from George I and George II?

_____

_____

_____

_____

_____

2. How do you think their family record might have affected him?

_____

_____

_____

_____

_____

3. How would the failures that Barbara Tuchman noted affect the way the British fought the war?

_____

_____

_____

_____

_____

Name_____ Date_____

CHALLENGES

1. Was George I a problem for Parliament? Why?

_____

_____

2. What title did George I hold before he became King of England?

_____

3. Who did Parliament use to keep control over George II?

_____

4. What relation was George III to George II?

_____

5. Why did George III like Lord North?

_____

_____

6. What title did Lord North refuse to accept?

_____

7. What two important military officers refused to fight the Americans?

_____

8. Why were British generals in contempt of Germain?

_____

_____

9. What has made the Earl of Sandwich famous today?

_____

_____

10. What did Admiral Barrington think of Sandwich and his friends at the Admiralty?

_____

_____

77

ADAMS, HENRY, & PAINE

It takes more than bad policy makers to create a revolution. As Jefferson wrote in the Declaration of Independence: "Mankind are more inclined to suffer, while evils are sufferable, than to right themselves by abolishing the forms to which they are accustomed." Revolutions don't just happen. Someone has to make them happen. In the colonies, three men were especially important in the early 1770s in creating tension, organizing resistance, and arousing people to act.

SAMUEL ADAMS (1722–1803), a Harvard graduate, was one of the worst financial managers in the colonies. His father loaned him £1,000 to start a business; he lost half of it in a bad debt to a friend and the rest by himself. He inherited his father's business, and it went broke. He became Boston's tax collector and did not collect the taxes to keep the city going. By the time he was 42 years old, his hair was gray and his hands trembled. His interest in politics, however, was making him a leader.

Samuel Adams led the colonists in Massachusetts in protests against the British.

As a member of the Caucus Club, a political group ranging from shipyard workers to intellectuals, he led the fight against the Stamp Act and Lieutenant Governor Hutchinson. During the battle over the Townsend Duties, he organized the Committee of Correspondence and the boycott. Other colonies imitated what Massachusetts was doing. He wrote articles for the *Boston Gazette,* and when Governor Bernard went to England, he declared a public festival with bonfires and roaring cannons. It was he who labelled the incident in Boston in 1770 as a "horrid massacre" and persuaded an engraver, Paul Revere, to make a cartoon showing soldiers shooting down unarmed civilians.

He was involved in organizing the Boston Tea Party and the call for a Continental Congress. When he went as a delegate, it was the first time in his life he had left Massachusetts. His friends fixed up his house and barn and gave him new clothes and shoes to wear.

The British did not know how to handle him. Although he was poor, he had no interest in money, so could not be bribed. Any attempt to arrest him would create a situation beyond Gage's control.

No one would have predicted greatness for PATRICK HENRY (1736–1799) as a young man. Since he hated picking tobacco worms off of leaves so much, his father gave him a store to run; it went broke. When he married, their parents gave the couple 300 acres of land and six slaves; the house burned, and he went back to running a store. It went broke. Without a way to support his wife, he turned to law, but he passed the bar exam only after he promised to study some more. When he appeared in his first big case, the jury members were amazed and awed by his presentation.

In 1765 he was elected to the House of Burgesses, where he sat with George Washington, Richard Henry Lee, and legal scholar George Wythe. He was almost alone in creating opposition to the Stamp Act, and the resolutions he offered were later toned down, but his reputation spread to other colonies as a man who stood up against royal authority. From 1767 to 1773, his law practice took most of his time. By 1773 he was thinking more about independence and ways to achieve it. He predicted that England would drive the colonies to rebellion; if that happened, France, Spain, and Holland (England's enemies) would support the American cause.

Henry was chosen as a delegate to the First Continental Congress where he gave a fiery speech: "The distinctions between Virginians, Pennsylvanians, New Yorkers and New Englanders are no more. I am not a Virginian, but an American." Another delegate, hearing Henry speak for the first time, called him "the completest speaker I ever heard," and looked forward to more examples of his ability. The crisis in Boston grew worse, and Virginia militia units began regular drills. Some Burgesses urged caution, but Henry said they were blind to painful truth, and closed his speech with the famous words: "Give me liberty or give me death!"

Growing up in a London slum with little love or money, THOMAS PAINE (1737–1809) was also a failure at everything he tried. His formal education at a charity school ended when he was 13, and he grew up in the streets and taverns. He married twice, but neither marriage lasted. Somehow, he met Benjamin Franklin, who wrote a letter of introduction for him: "Mr. Thomas Paine is very well recommended to me as an ingenious young man. He goes to Pennsylvania with a view of settling there." When the ship docked at Philadelphia, Paine was so sick he had to be carried off.

It was 1774, and the colonies were rapidly moving toward revolution. Paine caught the spirit of the times. He became a writer for the *Pennsylvania Magazine,* discussing topics from science to emancipation.

In January 1776, Paine's 47-page pamphlet, *Common Sense,* was published, and the chronic failure became an instant celebrity. In his pamphlet, Paine expressed his views on government: "Society in every state is a blessing, but Government, even in its best state, is but a necessary evil." Of the role of the king in England, he said: "A King hath little more to do than to make war and give away places; which in plain terms, is to impoverish the nation and set it together by the ears." *Common Sense* sold 120,000 copies in the first three months and about 500,000 in all.

Three men, all of whom had overcome failures, showed how different abilities worked together to create a revolution: Adams, the organizer; Henry, the public speaker; and Paine, the man with the poison pen. In the events from 1773 to 1776, their influence would be great.

Activity

Every revolution since the American Revolution has had its organizers, crowd stirrers, and writers. Have the class rate them in importance from 1 to 3.

Name_____ Date_____

POINTS TO PONDER

1. All three of these men were failures in their younger days. What effect do you think that had on their attitude toward England?

_____

_____

_____

_____

_____

_____

2. What does a good political speech need if it is going to move the listeners to action?

_____

_____

_____

_____

_____

3. What risks were Paine, Henry, and Adams running when they spoke out so strongly against English rule?

_____

_____

_____

_____

_____

_____

Name_____ Date_____

CHALLENGES

1. What public office had Samuel Adams held?

_____

2. What was the purpose of the Caucus Club?

_____

_____

3. What was Adams' response to Governor Bernard leaving the colony?

_____

4. Why didn't the British arrest Adams?

_____

_____

5. What issue first made Patrick Henry famous in other colonies?

_____

_____

6. Who did Henry think would come to the aid of the colonies in case of a war with England?

_____

7. What is probably Henry's most famous quote?

_____

_____

8. Who wrote a letter of introduction for Thomas Paine?

_____

9. What was Paine's first famous pamphlet?

_____

10. How many copies of that pamphlet were sold in the first three months?

_____

_____

BOSTON'S TEA PARTY (1771–1774)

Members of the Sons of Liberty dressed up as Mohawk Indians and dumped tea in Boston's harbor. The colonists had refused to buy tea from the East India Company in protest of the Tea Act of 1773.

The advertising campaign put on after the Boston Massacre by Samuel Adams, John Hancock, and Paul Revere was a great success. "Innocent Americans Gunned Down" would be the modern headline. This was a time for cool heads to work out problems, but those actively involved were not thinking about solving differences. They just wanted to make their points known.

Lord North became prime minister in January 1770 and saw that the Townsend Act was producing far less revenue than costs. The colonists were not importing British goods, and troops and royal officials were in danger. He proposed that the Townsend duties all be dropped, *except* for the tax on tea. He wanted to keep one tax in place to prove that England was strong. The boycott of British goods declined, and merchants felt free to import everything except tea. North felt he had made his point.

Samuel Adams suggested that his cousin, John Adams, run for the Massachusetts House. John's law practice was booming; if he ran, he knew it would cost him time and clients. His wife, Abigail, cried when he told her about Samuel's offer, but he accepted anyway. In his election, John Hancock was upset when told he had been re-elected by a vote of only 511–2, but after he was reminded that he had cast one of the votes against himself, he served anyway. The House chose Hancock for the governor's Council, but he refused the seat. That warned Governor Hutchinson that Hancock, the richest man in the colony, was not on his side.

Lieutenant William Dudingston, commander of the Royal Navy's ship, *Gaspee,* was also making a point when he tightened custom's patrols off Rhode Island. Dudingston was easy to hate, arrogant, insolent, and strict. Then the *Gaspee* ran aground seven miles from Providence. John Brown, a Providence merchant, now made his point. He gathered a group of men and sent them in longboats to the *Gaspee.* As the boarders prepared to climb on the ship, one of them shot Lieutenant Dudingston. Fortunately, a medical student was with the boarders and managed to save the lieutenant's life. After the crew was put in boats, the *Gaspee* was set afire and burned to the water line. In the naval inquiry that followed, the *Gaspee's* crew said that many of those who raided the ship were gentlemen.

In 1773 Parliament passed the TEA ACT. Its purpose was not to hurt Americans, in fact they were to benefit from it. The problem England faced was that one of its most important companies, the East India Company, was in danger of going broke. To help it get rid of surplus tea, the company was to sell tea to the colonists through special agents. The price to consumers would be cheaper than smuggled tea. It was American merchants like Hancock, and not their customers, who were upset by the Tea Act.

Resistance to the Tea Act began in New York and Philadelphia. The smugglers/ businessmen worked up opposition to the Tea Act by charging that it was the first step of a plot to give the East India Company control over all importing into the colonies and was a sneaky way to get Americans to accept the tea tax. New York's governor thought tea could be safely landed but was uncertain that it could ever be sold. In both instances, so much pressure was put on merchants who were to receive the tea that all backed off.

Samuel Adams saw this as an opportunity to make a point. Boston officials were warned by a large protest rally that it was unwise to take the cargo of 1,253 chests of tea off the ships. The ship captains wanted to sail to England with the tea, but Governor Hutchinson (who had a financial stake in selling the tea) would not let them. On December 16, 1773, Sons of Liberty dressed as Mohawk Indians boarded the ships and dumped the tea overboard. Care was taken to make sure no one carried any tea away. The ships' decks were cleaned, and the first mate on each ship signed a statement that no cargo except tea was taken. Bostonians sang: "Rally Mohawks! Bring out your axes, and tell King George, we'll pay no taxes." Some Americans rallied around this Boston Tea Party, but others did not like it, including Benjamin Franklin and George Washington, who feared it would cause the British to overreact.

INTOLERABLE ACTS. As predicted, Lord North used the Tea Party as reason to crack down on the hotbed of treason, Massachusetts. Five laws were passed to demonstrate that such actions would bring down the full wrath of the king. The Boston Port Act closed Boston's port until the tea was paid for. The Massachusetts Government Act gave the governor more power, including choosing the Council (it had always been elected). No town meetings could be held without the governor's permission. The Act for the Administration of Justice required that royal officials be tried in England or another colony if they could not receive a fair trial in local courts. The Quartering Act allowed all colonial governors to take whatever buildings were necessary to house British troops. The Quebec Act expanded Quebec to include the region north of the Ohio River and east of the Mississippi River (ignoring the claims of some of the 13 colonies to that land). Catholic priests in Quebec would be allowed to collect the tithe. French legal tradition was to replace English tradition in Quebec (eliminating jury trial). Hutchinson left Massachusetts to travel to England, and General Thomas Gage came to Boston to replace him, bringing four regiments of troops for company.

REACTION TO THE INTOLERABLE ACTS. Americans realized that if one colony could have its economy and self-government taken away by Parliament, the same thing might happen to their own colonies later. Even those who disapproved of the Tea Party thought England was going too far with their punishment.

It was time to meet and talk over how the colonies should respond. In September 1774, the First Continental Congress met in Philadelphia.

Activity

Hold a meeting of the Caucus Club after the tea tax was announced. Talk about some of the actions you might take, and after someone suggests a "tea party," talk about why dressing up like Mohawks seems a good idea.

Name_____ Date_____

POINTS TO PONDER

1. If Hancock had joined the Council, how would it have hurt him politically?

_____

_____

_____

_____

_____

_____

2. If you had been Dudingston, would you have testified against the men who boarded your ship? Why?

_____

_____

_____

_____

_____

3. What might have been a smarter way for Parliament to react to the Tea Party?

_____

_____

_____

_____

_____

Name_____ Date_____

CHALLENGES

1. Why did Lord North want to keep the tax on tea?

_____

_____

2. Why was Hancock upset about his election to the House?

_____

_____

3. Who was the only casualty in the *Gaspee* affair?

_____

4. Was the tea tax passed to punish American tea drinkers? What was the reason?

_____

_____

5. Who led the resistance to it?

_____

6. How much of the tea was sold in New York and Philadelphia?

_____

7. Why didn't Governor Hutchinson want the tea sent to England?

_____

_____

8. Why did Washington oppose the Tea Party?

_____

_____

9. Of the Intolerable Acts, which was going to hurt the Boston economy the most?

_____

_____

10. Who replaced Hutchinson as governor?

_____

DECLARING INDEPENDENCE (1774–1776)

It was one thing to feel that the Intolerable Acts were an evil injustice. It was quite another to decide what to do about it. Views ranged from declaring independence to keeping the status quo. This lack of agreement was obvious when the First Continental Congress met in Philadelphia in 1774. Eleven colonies were represented by 55 delegates.

The FIRST CONTINENTAL CONGRESS displayed the confu-

When signing the Declaration of Independence, delegates knew they would be risking their lives if America's attempt to break away from Britain failed.

sion Americans felt about how to react to Parliament's policies. Samuel Adams wanted independence, but was advised not to mention the "i" word for fear it might cause southern delegates to leave. On the other extreme, Reverend Jonathan Boucher of Virginia accepted without question Parliament's right to govern the empire and the American colonists' duty to obey.

Arguments were frequent, but people did not travel that far just to argue. The urge to decide something was strong. Pennsylvania's Joseph Galloway proposed creating a third house of Parliament, an American "grand council," with power to approve or reject actions by Parliament before they became law in the colonies. In local matters, each colonial legislature was to still make the laws. It seemed logical, but had no appeal to Patrick Henry or Samuel Adams. Henry warned it would lead a corrupt Parliament to corrupt Americans as well. Galloway's plan was tabled.

At the Suffolk county convention in Massachusetts, resolutions had been drawn up. These were considered and adopted by the congress. Among other things, they provided that: (1) the colonists were entitled to life, liberty, and property, (2) they should enjoy all rights of other English subjects, (3) keeping a standing army in any colony without its legislature's consent was illegal, and (4) the Intolerable Acts violated the colonists' rights. In parting, Congress voted to meet in May 1775 if all problems were not solved.

THE ASSOCIATION. Congress created a committee to cut off trade with England to protest British policies that were harmful to the colonists. Any merchants trading with England would answer to the "Association," and be "universally condemned as enemies of American liberty."

LEXINGTON AND CONCORD. Tension in Massachusetts was increasing, and General Gage's efforts to keep the situation under control were in vain. Committees of Safety were running the entire colony except Boston. Militia were also drilling and gathering arms and gunpowder. On April 19, 1775, Gage sent 1,000 troops to destroy supplies reportedly gathered at Lexington and Concord. Militia units that tried to stop them were easily brushed aside, but when the redcoats tried to return to Boston, their misery began.

By that time, militia had taken positions behind stone walls and fences and fired upon the king's troops all the way back. Each side blamed the other for opening fire and for commiting atrocities on the wounded and dead.

OTHER ACTIONS also took place in 1775. Militia commanded by Ethan Allen and Benedict Arnold captured Fort Ticonderoga, "in the name of Jehovah and the Continental Congress." The guns captured there were sent by sleigh to Boston. An attack on Montreal failed. The lack of Canadian support for the American cause was obvious. In June a British army under General Howe attacked colonial defenses built on Breed's Hill. This battle (mistakenly labelled as Bunker Hill) was won by the British at high cost in casualties and only on the third charge, after the militia were out of ammunition. Howe considered it the worst battle he had ever seen.

SECOND CONTINENTAL CONGRESS. As promised in 1774, if problems were not worked out in a year, another congress of the colonies was to be held. The Second Congress still didn't want war and expressed its loyalty to the king in the Olive Branch petition. Leaving nothing to chance, however, they voted to create a 20,000 man army and chose George Washington to lead it.

Events moved rapidly now. America learned the king had rented 30,000 German troops. Since many were from Hesse, they were all referred to as Hessians. The Iroquois of New York began to threaten frontier towns, and Americans believed the English were stirring them up. *Common Sense* was published, and its argument that an island should not rule a continent made common sense to many colonists. General William Howe (who replaced Gage) pulled troops out of Boston in the spring of 1776.

In Congress, a few still hoped problems with England could be worked out, but more were leaning toward independence. They knew the colonists could not defeat the British without help, and that help would not come unless the Americans made a clean break from England by declaring independence. On June 7, 1776, Richard Henry Lee proposed that "these United Colonies are, and of right ought to be, free and independent states." This caused a major debate, and many delegates sent an urgent message home asking for instructions (on how to vote). Finally, on July 2, 12 colonies voted in favor of the resolution. New York's delegates had to wait a week before being told they were to vote for independence.

In June Congress had appointed a five-man committee to write a Declaration of Independence. Among the members were Thomas Jefferson, Benjamin Franklin, and John Adams. The committee chose 33-year-old Jefferson to do the writing. He borrowed ideas from John Locke. To summarize the Declaration: (1) governments were created to protect the citizens' life, liberty, and pursuit of happiness; (2) if government threatened those rights, the people had a right to alter or abolish the government and replace it; (3) such changes were not to be made lightly; (4) the Americans had tried to work with England, but the English government had not listened; and (5) the king had repeatedly violated American rights, leaving no choice except to declare independence.

Activity

Assume various roles at the Second Congress. There should be someone who favors independence, someone who prefers the Galloway approach, and another who favors remaining loyal to the king. Discuss whether or not to declare independence.

Name_____ Date_____

POINTS TO PONDER

1. If the Galloway Plan had been adopted, what would the relationship between Americans and the British government be today?

_____

_____

_____

_____

_____

2. According to the Declaration of Independence, who had broken the unwritten "contract" between the king and his colonial subjects? How?

_____

_____

_____

_____

_____

3. Why was signing the Declaration of Independence a decision that, if things turned out wrong, could be fatal?

_____

_____

_____

_____

_____

Name_____ Date_____

CHALLENGES

1. What was the "i" word that Samuel Adams was not to mention? Why was he told not to mention it?

_____

_____

2. How would Jonathan Boucher and Patrick Henry get along? Why?

_____

_____

3. What was Galloway's third house of Parliament to be called? What was it to do?

_____

_____

4. What did the First Continental Congress think was wrong with the Intolerable Acts?

_____

_____

5. What was the purpose of the "Association"?

_____

_____

6. When did trouble really begin for British troops sent to Lexington and Concord?

_____

7. What did the attack on Montreal indicate?

_____

8. What nickname did all German troops go by?

_____

9. Who proposed independence?

_____

10. Who were three members of the committee that wrote the Declaration of Independence? Underline the one actually doing the writing.

_____

WASHINGTON: SYMBOL OF THE REVOLUTION

The Second Congress faced the question of who should lead its army. John Hancock wanted the honor, but instead, eyes turned toward a tall, muscular man wearing a Virginia militia uniform. During his lifetime, eyes always seemed to turn toward George Washington.

It was almost as if his whole life prepared him for the role of leading an army, and later, a nation. The first Washington, John, came to Virginia in 1675, 57 years before the birth of his grandson, George. Augustine Washington (George's father) married twice; George was the first son of the second wife. Augustine hoped his sons would study in England, but he died when George was 11. Augustine was not wealthy, and the most important thing he left his son was the responsibility for the care of his mother and four brothers and sisters. As a boy

Although Washington did not want to be general in chief of the Continental Army, he proved to be an excellent commander during the trying years of the Revolution.

he adopted 110 rules of conduct to live by. Two examples were: "Sleep not when others speak, sit not when others stand, speak not when you should hold your peace" and "Undertake not what you cannot perform but be careful to keep your promise."

George's half-brother, Lawrence, had the most impact on George's life. Lawrence served as an officer in an American unit during a war with Spain and had taken part in the capture of the West Indian fort of Cartagena. Lawrence taught his eager younger brother the manual of arms and excited his interest in serving in the king's army. George spent a short time in school and learned some Latin, but most of his education was outdoors. He was a skilled surveyor by the age of 14.

When he was 16, George went with a surveying expedition into frontier country. Surveying for others and buying land for himself took Washington out to the frontier many times and gave him an understanding of western affairs that few planters had. It also taught him how to survive a cold night's sleep under a bear blanket covered with lice and fleas.

Lawrence died when George was 20, and Washington inherited his estate at Mount Vernon. Running a plantation was like running a town; there were hired workers, overseers, and slaves to supervise. Washington was responsible for seeing that the community was well fed, clothed, and housed. He loved farming and noted that crops grew better in some soils on his land than others. He set up a crude laboratory to test his theories. Washington was a detail man, keeping careful notes and records.

In 1753 Washington was appointed major in the Virginia militia. Governor Dinwiddie sent him on the trips west that resulted in war with France. At Fort Necessity, Washington learned what it was like to be shot at. Washington went with Braddock's expedition as a volunteer, and he and the Virginia militia covered the retreat. Washington hoped his courage on that occasion would win him a high-ranking officer's position in the British army. It did not.

Instead, he faced the difficult task of protecting Virginia's long frontier with only a handful of men.

During the French and Indian War, he was often in the thick of battles, sometimes riding back and forth between the two armies. Horses were shot out from under him, but he somehow escaped being wounded. He appeared healthy, but at different times, was deathly ill. The British never gave him the respect he deserved or the officer's commission that he wanted.

In 1759 Washington resigned as colonel of the Virginia militia and happily returned to civilian life. He met and married Martha, the widow of Dan Custis. She had received a large part of the Custis estate, and between them, they owned 200 slaves. Washington considered slavery a poor way to get work done, but he did not sell his slaves. As a result, he had more than he needed. The Washingtons entertained many guests at Mt. Vernon and, when they could, went to the theater and dances at Williamsburg. Washington also enjoyed fox hunts and took great interest in his horses and hunting dogs.

By 1769 Washington's patience with England was wearing thin. He had grown to dislike English ways: the way he and other colonial officers had been treated as inferiors and personal irritation with the way his business agents in London were treating him. After attending the First Continental Congress, he left feeling that war was coming. As a delegate to the Second Congress, he wore his military uniform to indicate Virginia's willingness to fight if a war must be fought. Washington did not want to be the general in chief. But when the position was offered to him, he accepted.

There were certain characteristics that made Washington what James Flexner called: "the indispensable man." (1) He had the courage of his convictions. Once he decided something was right, he held to it. During the war, Congress often gave him very little support. A weaker man would have quit, and a stronger man would have seized power as dictator; Washington never considered either temptation.

(2) He learned from his mistakes. Like the rest of his army, he went through on-the-job training that included learning who was capable and who was not. Some officers came with imposing military records, but when he discovered they could not fight, they were cast aside. His own abilities grew as he fought the war. He developed an effective spy network that kept him well informed. He made mistakes but kept the respect of his best officers and enlisted men through "times that try men's souls" as Thomas Paine put it.

(3) He set examples for his troops. His eye for detail required that he dress properly, avoid too much friendliness with his officers and men, show no fear on the battlefield, remind the men at times why they were fighting, and most difficult for him, keep his temper under control.

Activity

Washington was almost idolized by Americans for many years after his death in 1799. How can individuals such as Washington change history? Did Washington become a hero because of great or small decisions? To what extent do famous people have an obligation to set an example?

Name_____ Date_____

POINTS TO PONDER

1. *Noblesse oblige* [nobless' oblezh] is the responsibility of the upper class to set an example of honorable conduct. What were some examples of that in Washington's conduct?

_____

_____

_____

_____

_____

2. What were some of the "bad" things that happened to Washington that worked to his advantage in the long run?

_____

_____

_____

_____

_____

3. How did some of his characteristics have a great effect on everything that has happened to the United States since his time?

_____

_____

_____

_____

_____

Name_____ Date_____

CHALLENGES

1. What responsibility did Augustine Washington lay on his son?

_____

_____

2. How many rules did George Washington try to live by?

_____

3. Who taught George Washington about military affairs?

_____

4. What plantation did George Washington inherit?

_____

5. What important role did Washington have in the Braddock expedition?

_____

_____

6. What was his wife's name before they married?

_____

7. How many slaves did the Washingtons own? How did he feel about slavery?

_____

_____

8. When did Washington first feel war was coming?

_____

9. What did he wear to sessions of the Second Continental Congress?

_____

_____

10. How did Washington keep informed on British movements?

_____

_____

WEIGHING THE ODDS

How can we win? In any contest (and war is a contest), each side looks at its strengths (assets) and tries to find ways to take advantage of the other side's weaknesses (liabilities). The 13 colonies had never worked well together before, but as Benjamin Franklin said, "We must indeed all hang together, or, most assuredly, we shall all hang separately." From the beginning, they counted on French and Spanish support, because they knew both countries hated England. They also knew that England had been at war nearly 90 years, and the public was tired of financing wars. They believed that if they could wear the English down, American independence would become a reality.

Both Continental and Militia troops gained experience as the war went on. Fighting for their homes, families, and their freedom gave them the incentive to face one of the greatest armies in the world.

ARMIES. The <u>British army</u> was truly professional. Its enlisted men expected to serve until they were too old to campaign or died. The officers were aristocrats who lived well and spent their time drinking, gambling, and enjoying the company of the ladies.

Enlisted men were "recruited" by search parties who went through prisons, bars, and lower-class neighborhoods and picked up criminals, drunks, and vagrants. These were taken to camp where they were beaten and lashed into obedient soldiers. Nothing the enlisted man did required thinking. Marching and drilling were all by command. They marched onto the battlefield in close order, wedged against the man on either side, formed three or four lines, and fired in volleys. It required seven commands to shoot their muskets. Since muskets had a range of only 100 yards, the armies stood close to each other. After a few volleys, a bayonet charge often followed.

It was common practice to rent troops from rulers who were not at war. Europe's wars were not fought in winter or in rain. Battles were fought in open fields. Soldiers were not fighting for "king and country," but for the small salary, bad food, and ale they were provided.

<u>Patriot troops</u>. Washington wanted to build an army with able officers and disciplined troops. In battle, he had two groups available to him. *Continentals* were Washington's professional army. Paid $7 a month in Continental currency, they moved from one state to another and one battlefield to another. At first, they fought badly, but by the end of the war, thanks to experience and training by Baron von Steuben and other European officers, they held their own with some of England's best soldiers.

Militia were state troops led by officers they had elected. Militia had little training and in battle were unreliable. Like the Continentals, they were not easily ordered around. Tactics had to be kept simple, and officers had to explain why they were doing a certain movement. For all their amateur ways, militia could and did fight well on occasion. The defense of their state, family, and property was incentive for them to fight.

POLITICAL STRENGTH. <u>Britain</u>. The king was determined to win, as were his chief advisors. However, George III had many enemies anxious to cut the king down to size and restore Parliament to its position before he had decided to "be king." As the war lingered on after Saratoga, taxpayers grew restless and wanted to make peace with the Americans.

<u>America</u> had no ruler; the Second Continental Congress was just a committee at first. At times, Congress showed backbone, as when it voted to create an army and send diplomats to Europe. Without the authority to tax or draft troops, however, most of its time was spent deciding which general to promote, begging states and foreign nations for money, and ignoring urgent appeals from Washington for supplies and payment for his men. As the British troops moved in their direction, they packed to leave. Some in Congress were a help, others were easily discouraged.

Public opinion in America fell into three general categories. *Patriots* supported independence, *neutrals* took no position, and *loyalists* favored returning to English rule. Patriots were divided between radicals, who wanted a social revolution making everyone equal, and conservatives, who were only interested in freedom from English rule. Neutrals were those who opposed wars (pacifists) and those who wished the whole storm would go away. Loyalists, because of tradition or some economic tie, remained loyal to the King. Usually, they kept their views to themselves until the British army appeared, and then they announced their loyalty. When the British left, many loyalists went with them. During the war, about 50,000 loyalists joined the British army as volunteers wearing forest green uniforms.

ECONOMIC RESOURCES. England had a clear advantage. Their money was accepted without question, their production was much higher, and they could afford to rent armies from German princes. America was short on gold and silver, its continental currency became a joke, and it lacked the capacity to produce enough military supplies to meet the needs of the army. Americans began making cannons in 1775, but most had to be imported. In only one area of arms-making did Americans excel, and that was in Kentucky (or Pennsylvania) rifles. With them, Daniel Morgan's sharpshooters were able to pick off British officers at long distances.

OTHER FACTORS. <u>England</u> faced a number of problems. The Irish were rebellious, so the king needed to keep a large army there. France, Spain, and Holland were hostile and could take advantage of England if the Admiralty sent too many ships away. The Dutch and French islands in the Atlantic were storage depots for supplies heading to the United States.

<u>Patriots</u> certainly had their problems, too. Many merchants and farmers were more willing to supply the English army that paid them in gold and silver than Continentals who paid them in paper money. Washington's ragtag army was short on everything; one soldier described his supper as a "leg of nothing and no turnips." That kind of diet discouraged all but the most committed. By the end of the war, that devotion would make the difference.

Activity

Make a chart showing the strengths and weaknesses of each side. You should include those that were not mentioned such as distance of supply sources, difficulties of receiving information and orders, knowledge of terrain, attitudes of the people, and so on.

Name_____ Date_____

POINTS TO PONDER

1. What part does politics play in a war?

_____

_____

_____

_____

_____

_____

2. Why did the English and European armies use such harsh discipline?

_____

_____

_____

_____

_____

_____

3. As a loyalist, why would you not let everyone know where you stood?

_____

_____

_____

_____

_____

_____

Name_____ Date_____

CHALLENGES

1. Who did the Americans expect to help them?

_____

2. Why did the Americans think the British could not fight a long war?

_____

_____

3. Where did the British go to find enlisted men for their army?

_____

4. How many commands did it take before an English soldier fired his musket? What was the musket's range?

_____

_____

5. What improved the quality of Continentals?

_____

_____

6. What inspired militia to fight?

_____

_____

7. When did British opinion turn against continuing the war?

_____

8. What did radical patriots want?

_____

_____

9. How could loyalists be spotted on a battlefield?

_____

_____

10. What weapon did the Americans have that was superior to English muskets?

_____

EARLY STAGES OF THE WAR (1776–1777)

War is a game best played down the middle of the field. If you move too far toward the side of caution or veer toward impulsive actions, you may well lose even if your army has all the advantage on its side.

Despite early defeats in New York, Washington's surprise victories in the winter of 1776–1777 bolstered the morale of the patriot army.

After General Howe's redcoats left Boston in March 1776, no British troops occupied the colonies for a time. This gave the Second Congress the time it needed to declare independence and set up operations. Washington had no spy network yet and could only guess where and when Howe would return. He gambled that Howe would pick New York City. Washington moved his headquarters to New York and stationed men on Long Island and Manhattan.

In 1776 Germain sent plans for a three-pronged attack. General Carleton was to move down from Canada and take Albany; General William Howe was to capture New York; General Henry Clinton was to move by sea to attack the Carolinas where loyalist sentiment was said to be strong. Things did not go as planned, however. Carleton was stalled by a patriot fleet on Lake Champlain commanded by General Benedict Arnold. By the time Clinton arrived in the South, patriots had silenced the loyalists. Clinton then sailed north to join Howe.

Washington's mistakes of dividing his forces, failing to develop cavalry, and sometimes leaving flanks uncovered made it easier for the British to defeat him on Long Island, Manhattan, and at White Plains. For Washington, this was a dark time. His troops were deserting, Congress was not supporting him, and his second in command, General Charles Lee, wanted to replace him. When Lee was captured by the British and held prisoner for 18 months, it was a blessing not visible at the time. Washington's ever-decreasing army moved to New Jersey. Howe divided his army, with outposts on the east side of the Delaware River. It was winter 1776, a time for armies to rest around their stoves. No one fights in blizzards.

Washington, the fox hunter, now knew how a fox felt when chased from one hole to another by the hounds. It seemed like Howe was toying with him. Washington did something no European general would consider. Instead of waiting until spring when superior British forces could run him down, he planned an attack in the cold of winter.

Crossing the Delaware River, moving boats through the chunks of ice, his men struck the Hessian outpost at Trenton on Christmas Day 1776. The drunken Hessian commander paid no attention to a note warning that the Americans were approaching. The attack was swift and successful; 918 barely-awake Hessians raised their hands in surrender. After moving his captives to Pennsylvania, Washington advanced on Princeton. His army met a British force under General Cornwallis near Trenton, but Cornwallis chose to drink rather than attack. He would bag the fox tomorrow. That night, Washington's men moved around

Cornwallis's flank and attacked British troops near Princeton. Cornwallis withdrew to protect his supply base. The New Jersey campaigns greatly restored patriot hopes.

In 1777 "Coach" Germain sent new instructions, again calling for a three-pronged attack. Howe was to advance northward from New York. Barry St. Leger was to attack Oswego, New York, and move eastward down the Mohawk valley. John Burgoyne was to move down Lake Champlain and join the other forces at Albany. Once again, the campaign did not come off as planned.

HOWE. General Howe's girlfriend, Mrs. Joshua Loring, persuaded him that Philadelphia was more fun than New York. He received permission from Germain to attack Philadelphia, the rebel capital. With Howe's forces nearby and Washington unable to stop them at Brandywine Creek, Congress moved to Lancaster, Pennsylvania, in September 1777. Howe wined and dined in Philadelphia while Washington's men froze and starved at Valley Forge.

ST. LEGER. Barry St. Leger was a young colonel who arrived in western New York with 500 redcoats and Hessians, 500 loyalists, and 1,000 Indians led by the Mohawk chief, Joseph Brandt. He laid siege to Fort Stanwix, defended by General Nicholas Herkimer. Efforts to capture the old fort failed. During the siege, a runner escaped the fort and reached General Benedict Arnold. Quickly raising an army, Arnold headed toward Fort Stanwix, and then he happened to find Hon Yost. The Yosts were loyalists, and Hon's brother was about to be executed. Arnold offered a deal to him; Yost's brother would be spared if Yost persuaded St. Leger's Mohawks that a large force was on its way. Yost did his part, and the scared Indians left. St. Leger had to turn back.

BURGOYNE. Burgoyne's march south was almost leisurely at first. He easily captured Ticonderoga, but from there, progress became more difficult. He carried too many supply wagons and cannons with him and had to build bridges when he came to rivers. He sent a Hessian colonel to Vermont to recruit loyalists and get supplies, but they were stopped by General John Stark's 2,600 recently-recruited men, who attacked them near Bennington and killed or captured almost all of them. General Horatio Gates, in command of U.S. forces in New York, found new volunteers coming to his camp each day. While Howe feasted in Philadelphia and St. Leger's men fled for their lives toward Lake Ontario, the trap was about to spring.

In September 1777, Burgoyne crossed to the west side of the Hudson River. At Freeman's Farm, Daniel Morgan and Henry Dearborn's men held him back. In October, he was defeated at Bemis Heights, thanks to fearless actions by Benedict Arnold. Trapped, Burgoyne surrendered 5,700 men to Gates at Saratoga on October 17, 1777. In London and Paris, the news hit like an earthquake. This was the opportunity Benjamin Franklin had been waiting for.

Activity

Washington attacked Trenton in a blinding snowstorm on Christmas Day. Besides having to persuade men to leave warmth to cross a dangerous river in freezing temperatures, list other problems he faced in making such a move.

Name_____ Date_____

POINTS TO PONDER

1. It is important for armies to have "game plans" so they can work together on different fronts at the same time. Why didn't that work for Germain's plans?

_____

_____

_____

_____

_____

2. Of the British generals, which were more victims of their own mistakes, and which were victims of circumstances beyond their control?

_____

_____

_____

_____

_____

_____

3. What changes in morale do you think patriots went through in 1776–1777?

_____

_____

_____

_____

_____

_____

Name_____ Date_____

CHALLENGES

1. Where did Washington expect the English to land?

_____

2. What stopped Carleton's advance?

_____

_____

3. Why did Clinton fail in the Carolinas?

_____

_____

4. What was unusual about Washington's attack on Trenton?

_____

_____

5. Who missed an opportunity to defeat Washington near Trenton when he returned to New Jersey?

_____

6. As Germain planned it, where would British armies meet in 1777?

_____

7. Why might Howe have presented a case for taking Philadelphia?

_____

_____

8. Whose help made it possible for Arnold to weaken the British force at Fort Stanwix?

_____

9. Why did Burgoyne have to build bridges?

_____

_____

10. What three generals were important in Gates' victory at Saratoga?

_____

THE DIPLOMATIC WAR

Benjamin Franklin was very popular as ambassador to France. After the American victory at Saratoga, he was able to negotiate a treaty with France that included open trade and recognition as an independent nation.

The United States boldly declared itself a new nation on July 4, 1776. To make that dream come true required success on the battlefield, where cannons and muskets ruled. For those cannons and muskets to roar required cannonballs and gunpowder. The new nation produced only a small quantity of either. For Washington to succeed, he needed supplies from the outside. To be recognized as independent by other nations is very important to a revolution; otherwise, the rebels are nothing more than traitors and bandits. Bandits get no help, and nations despise traitors. The new United States needed supplies and respect to win the Revolution.

Great Britain had strutted proudly since the Seven Years' War ended in 1763. The country had humiliated France and Spain. For the French, who had been on top a century before, and the Spanish, on top two centuries before, English arrogance was hard to take. French Foreign Minister Vergennes was anxious for revenge. He was well aware of the troubles in the colonies after the Stamp Act and delighted in news of American acts of defiance.

Vergennes was a cautious man. A mistake could be fatal to France. It had quietly rebuilt its navy and army since 1763, but it was still no match for England. He could not openly supply the Americans or express his support for them. But if he could find secret ways to help and let them know France was in their corner, he would do it. Spain had not liked England since the Battle of the Spanish Armada, so they had a reason to help their ally, France. But Spain also had colonies; if the United States succeeded, their colonies might revolt. Spain's king, Charles III, was never rushed. His policy was always slow and careful. The Dutch carried on a very profitable trade with Americans from their port at St. Eustatius in the Dutch West Indies. Three nations watched and waited to see what happened in North America.

In November 1775, Congress created a secret committee to contact England's enemies. The first two diplomats appointed were not very good. Arthur Lee was in England at the time; he used the code name "Mary Johnston," which must have amused the British spies he hired as clerks. Silas Deane disguised himself as "Jones," and even though he spoke little French, he was to serve as "commercial agent" to France. After independence was declared, three far more important diplomats were sent: Benjamin Franklin to France, John Jay to Spain, and John Adams to England.

Franklin arrived in Paris in December 1776. His *Poor Richard's Almanack* had been translated into French, and rich and poor alike laughed at his humor. Scientists admired his work with electricity, his invention of bifocal eyeglasses, and his new stove. Franklin had an actor's flair for the dramatic, often wearing a fur cap and the humble clothing of an American farmer. He was a celebrity, and his picture appeared on jewelry and watches. He mixed charm, humility, humor, and clever diplomacy to win the French public opinion.

Help was secretly given to the United States through a phony company, Hortalez et Compagnie. Military supplies were sent to the United States on 14 ships. American privateers (privately owned ships licensed to raid commerce) used French ports to sell their cargoes taken from English ships. After the English complained, the French usually ordered the privateer to leave, but by then, the cargo was sold. France helped, but Vergennes could not give what Franklin wanted almost as much: recognition.

Saratoga changed that. Lord North decided to offer the colonies self-rule within the empire. He sent Paul Wentworth to Paris to offer Franklin dominion status for America. Vergennes' spies knew that Wentworth and Franklin were meeting. Everything Vergennes hoped for might disappear if the United States and England patched up their differences. Vergennes offered Franklin a better deal: a *Treaty of Amity and Commerce* allowing the United States to openly trade with France. Vergennes knew the English would see this as grounds for war. A *Treaty of Alliance* was signed; if war broke out between England and France because of the other treaty, the United States and France promised to fight until the United States was given its freedom.

Both the English and French offers reached Congress at the same time. England offered everything *except* independence; the French offer *included* independence. Congress accepted the French offer in May 1778.

While Franklin was the "toast of Paris," John Jay suffered in Madrid. Jay had given up his successful law practice to serve his country. In the Spanish capital, he seemed unable to get anything done. Spanish officials kept delaying action, and all he accomplished there was a $150,000 loan. Jay developed a suspicion of all European diplomacy.

John Adams went to Holland in 1780. The Dutch were very successful in business matters. Their port of St. Eustatius was the stop-off for thousands of ships smuggling supplies into America. In December 1780, England declared war on Holland. Admiral Rodney took his British fleet to St. Eustatius and caught the Dutch off guard. Hundreds of Dutch and French ships were captured by the surprise attack. While Rodney enjoyed counting his loot in the Dutch West Indies, a French fleet under Admiral de Grasse sailed out of the islands to aid the American army collecting around Cornwallis's troops at Yorktown.

After Yorktown, the British knew they had lost. Lord North resigned, and Rockingham replaced him. Richard Oswald, a businessman friend of Franklin, was sent to Paris to see what terms might be made with the United States. Franklin knew he had the British in his hands now. Feeling the pains of old age, Franklin asked Jay and Adams to join him in working out peace terms.

Activity

Cryptograms substituting one letter for another were commonly used by American diplomats during the Revolution. Have part of the class write a secret message based on this lesson for the rest of the class to translate.

Name_____ Date_____

POINTS TO PONDER

1. Imagine that Alaskans are so angry with the United States that they declare independence. Russia wants to help them. What lessons could the Russians learn from French actions during the American Revolution?

_____

_____

_____

_____

_____

2. Silas Deane sent messages written in invisible ink. What ways do modern spies have of communicating?

_____

_____

_____

_____

_____

3. Why was Franklin so much more successful than any other diplomat would have been? Should celebrities be used as diplomats?

_____

_____

_____

_____

CHALLENGES

Name_____ Date_____

1. Who was the French foreign minister? How did he feel about England?

_____

_____

2. When did Spain's dislike for England begin?

_____

_____

3. Why was Spain reluctant to help Americans gain independence?

_____

_____

4. Who were the first two American diplomats appointed by Congress?

_____

5. What did scientists admire about Franklin?

_____

6. What was the business of Hortalez et Compagnie?

_____

_____

7. Why was Paul Wentworth sent to France?

_____

_____

8. What was the purpose of the Treaty of Amity and Commerce?

_____

9. How long did the Treaty of Alliance require that France and the United States fight England?

_____

10. What did de Grasse do while Rodney was in the Dutch West Indies?

_____

THE NAVAL WAR

John Paul Jones captained the newly-built, 18-gun ship, the *Ranger*, in 1777. It was the first ship to fly the new American flag.

Wars in the 18th century were usually fought for greed, not for noble causes. To take another nation's land or trade, to loot cities, and to make a country pay tribute for losing a war were good reasons for fighting. Individuals also looked for opportunities to gain through war. Navies enjoyed capturing enemy merchant ships because the booty was divided among the crew members. Privately owned merchant ships were converted to warships by arming them with guns; sailing with a license (letter of marque and reprisal), these privateers became legal pirates.

As the modern person thinks about the Revolution, thoughts rarely turn to ships. We should remind ourselves that (1) the American colonies were stretched out along the Atlantic, and rivers and the ocean were the main highways. If those highways were blocked, all economic movement stopped. (2) The United States depended on foreign supplies carried on ships to fight the war. (3) Lake Champlain and Lake Ontario were possible invasion routes and had to be protected by both forts and ships.

Navies of that time were all basically the same, but some ships were bigger or better built than others. Ships of the line had three decks of usually 64 to 74 guns; frigates typically had two decks of 42 to 44 guns; corvettes and sloops had one deck and were usually armed with 18 and 22 guns, respectively. The guns on a ship of the line were capable of firing cannon balls that weighed 12 to 42 pounds one mile. Frigates were armed with 4- to 6-pound cannons. It took at least two minutes for the best crews to load and fire.

The captain's role was very important for success or failure in a battle. He needed to take advantage of wind and currents to position his ship where it could use its firepower most effectively. Maneuvering these ships was not easy, and sailors who knew their jobs made the difference.

Under Lord Sandwich, the Royal Navy had declined since the Seven Years' War. Many ships were rotting and in poor condition, and even new ships were not as well constructed because of corruption in the Admiralty. The French navy, led by Duc de Choiseul, was building new ships and training professional ship-builders and naval officers. The *Marine Francaise* was not equal to the Royal Navy, but had a grudge to settle for earlier defeats at England's hand. Dutch naval power was not what it had been from 1652 to 1674 when it had fought the British for control of the English Channel.

In 1775 Congress created the navy and marine corps. Its first two ships were converted merchant ships: the 24-gun *Alfred* and 20-gun *Columbus.* States often had their own navies to bring in supplies and raid English shipping. There were also privateers, like the *Rattlesnake*, which captured over $1 million worth of goods while raiding the Baltic Sea. Both the navy and privateers raided British shipping. The *Reprisal* captured two ships while taking Benjamin Franklin to France.

Of U.S. captains, the best known was John Paul Jones. Born in Scotland, he sailed on British ships until he came to America in 1773. Jones served for a time on the *Alfred,* then was given command of the newly-built, 18-gun *Ranger* in 1777. The *Ranger* was the first ship to fly the new American flag and the first to be saluted by the crew of a foreign nation. Jones raided along the British coast and captured the *Drake,* a small British navy ship. In 1779 he was given command of a five-ship fleet that included the 40-gun *Bonhomme Richard* ("Poor Richard" in English, named for Benjamin Franklin's almanac) and the 36-gun frigate, the *Alliance.* Off Yorkshire, *Richard* and *Alliance* attacked the 54-gun *Serapis.* The ships were so close that Jones lashed his ship to the *Serapis,* but the situation seemed hopeless. An officer, hearing the false rumor that Jones had been killed, asked if they had surrendered. Jones shouted back: "I have not yet begun to fight." The *Serapis* commander finally surrendered. Efforts to save *Richard* failed, and Jones shifted his crew to the *Serapis.*

After returning to the United States, Jones was offered command of a 72-gun ship under construction, the *America,* but he never got his ship. He went to France, then Denmark, and finally to Russia, where Catherine the Great made him a rear admiral. He died in France in 1792.

War broke out between England and France in 1778 and between England and Spain in 1779. The French fleet had already been of great help to the United States during the war. Admiral D'Estaing forced the British out of Philadelphia and Newport and threatened British ships blockading the U.S. coast. Now, France and Spain formed a fleet of 66 ships to attack England across the English Channel. However, a calm that caused sails to hang limp, an epidemic, and a shortage of drinking water prevented the attack from occurring.

Rear Admiral George Rodney left England in 1774 because he was concerned that gambling debts might cause him to be thrown in debtors' prison. He was in France when the American Revolution broke out. Rodney returned to England in 1778 in hope of returning to naval service. A year later, Sandwich finally gave him a fleet to attack the West Indies. On his way, he defeated a Spanish fleet besieging Gibralter. Rodney was in the West Indies when he learned that England was at war with Holland, and the navy recommended he attack St. Eustatius. He surprised the island and gathered an enormous amount of wealth. While basking in his great fortune, he ignored the rumor that a large French fleet was heading his way.

Comte de Grasse moved out of the West Indies and sailed toward Virginia in August with 28 ships of the line and transports carrying three West Indies regiments. The noose was tightening at Yorktown.

Activity

Try to build a sailing ship from a model kit. You may come out of the experience with a greater appreciation for the problems facing ship builders of the time.

Name_____ Date_____

POINTS TO PONDER

1. How did having Lord Sandwich in charge of the British navy help the United States?

_____

_____

_____

_____

_____

2. What problems would privateers create if nations still used them?

_____

_____

_____

_____

_____

_____

3. Admiral Rodney was proud of his work in cleaning out St. Eustatius. Should he have been?

_____

_____

_____

_____

_____

_____

Name_____ Date_____

CHALLENGES

1. Why did navies especially enjoy capturing merchant ships?

_____

_____

2. What were two potential inland water routes for invasion?

_____

3. How would you recognize a ship of the line in a picture?

_____

_____

4. What was meant by a "42-pound cannon"?

_____

_____

5. Who was pushing ship construction for the *Marine Francaise?*

_____

6. What were the first two ships in the U.S. navy?

_____

7. What was an example of a successful privateer?

_____

8. What was the first U.S. ship John Paul Jones captained?

_____

9. What was the most famous naval battle of the American Revolution? Underline the U.S. ship's name.

_____

10. Who was admiral of the French fleet that sailed to Yorktown?

_____

_____

THE ROAD TO YORKTOWN

The saying goes: "It's not over till it's over." For Washington's English opponents, there were times when it looked like their victory was almost certain, but then Washington would slip from the trap.

The winter of 1777–1778 was spent by Washington's Continentals at Valley Forge, west of Philadelphia. To describe what the troops actually possessed required a much shorter list than the one for things they needed: food, shoes,

Suffering from a series of defeats and cut off from retreat by the French fleet, General Cornwallis surrendered his army to Washington on October 19, 1781.

coats, blankets, and gloves for starters. General Howe's warm, well-fed army enjoyed the winter in Philadelphia. Farmers brought wagon-loads of supplies to the British, who paid in gold and silver. Privateers raided English ships and captured boots, but they were stored in warehouses until they mildewed. Congress paid little attention to pleas from the army for food and supplies. Men deserted, not because they were unpatriotic, but because they were starving. This was no time for Thomas Paine's "sunshine patriot."

Many foreign officers had come to help the Americans, including the Marquis de Lafayette, but most had made little difference. During that cold winter at Valley Forge, Baron von Steuben arrived and took on the job of teaching Washington's men the fine arts of drilling and fighting. He was good tonic for the army; Steuben combined discipline with humor. When his men drilled badly, he swore at them in German, and when he realized they did not understand anything he said, he had an officer swear at them in English. By the end of the year, they were enthusiastic about drills and eager to test what they had learned on the English.

In 1778 General Clinton replaced Howe and began moving his army from Philadelphia to New York. Some redcoats went by ship, but 10,000 went overland. Washington sent General Charles Lee (who had been released by the British) to attack Clinton at Monmouth while his men were stretched in a long line. An attack began, but Lee suddenly ordered a retreat. Washington arrived just in time and turned the army around. Defenses held when the British troops hit their line. Both sides had about 350 casualties. Lee was later court-martialed and removed from the army. Clinton captured New York City, and Washington built his defenses at White Plains to the north.

Eastern Pennsylvania and western New York were hit by violent loyalist-Indian raids in 1778. Many Kentucky settlers left for safer ground east of the mountains. George Rogers Clark became important, not only for holding the west, but for putting the English on the defensive there. In 1776 he persuaded Virginia to give him 500 pounds of gunpowder to protect Kentucky, and in 1777 he led the militia that saved Harrodsburg from Indian attack. In 1778–1779, Clark's handful of men criss-crossed the west several times, forcing the

English and Indians to defend themselves instead of going on the offensive. When he returned with "Hairbuyer" Colonel Henry Hamilton as his prisoner, westerners breathed easier.

Washington not only had to watch Clinton, but had to keep an eye on some in his own army. A group of officers in 1777 felt that Gates should be appointed to replace Washington. Washington demolished that "Conway Cabal" (cabal is a group of plotters) by quoting what one of them said in a letter. Gates was greatly embarrassed. Washington even had trouble with his aide, Colonel Alexander Hamilton, who left the army for a while because Washington criticized him for lateness. Mutinies became more frequent when food was reduced or old timers in the army felt that new enlistees were receiving undeserved bonuses.

Benedict Arnold's treason was the greatest blow to Washington. It resulted from several things: his love for a loyalist woman (Peggy Shippen) whom he married, living above his income, being passed over for promotion by Congress, and charges that he abused his powers. Arnold persuaded Washington to make him the commander at West Point and arranged for Clinton to send a spy (Major John Andre) to work out a deal. In their plot, Arnold was to surrender West Point to the English in return for a brigadier general's commission, a bonus, and a pension for his wife. Andre, dressed in civilian clothes, was captured and hanged; Arnold fled to British lines, leaving his wife behind to proclaim she had no idea what her husband was doing. Arnold fought as a loyalist for the rest of the war and went to England afterward.

The war shifted to the South in 1778, where Cornwallis's British captured Savannah in 1778 and Charleston in 1780. General Gates was sent to punish the British intruders, but he lost at Camden, South Carolina, in 1780 and was replaced by a better general, Nathaniel Greene. Combining against the British were such fighters as Daniel Morgan and his sharpshooters, Francis Marion, the "Swamp Fox," and the cavalry of "Lighthorse" Harry Lee and Lewis Washington. In one battle after another, the British were taking a beating. General Cornwallis was almost in shock after the lopsided losses at King's Mountain and Cowpens. He had counted on loyalist support, but loyalist units disappeared almost as quickly as they were recruited.

Cornwallis moved toward the Virginia coastline, hoping that the Royal Navy would take them away. French general Rochambeau and Washington asked Admiral de Grasse to bring his fleet to Yorktown. The French fleet and an army of 16,000 men had cut Cornwallis off from any more retreats. On October 19, 1781, Cornwallis surrendered.

When news of Yorktown reached London, Lord North said: "Oh God, it is all over." North resigned and was replaced by Lord Rockingham, who had always thought the war was a mistake. It was not quite over, however. General Guy Carleton, who had replaced Clinton, remained in New York until ordered home in December 1783. Then at last, the war was ended.

Activity

Look up one of the American or British officers included in this section. Then write clues for others in the class to use to find the right person.

Name_____ Date_____

POINTS TO PONDER

1. Thomas Paine had written: "These are the times that try men's souls." What kind of problems did Washington face that might have broken most men?

_____

_____

_____

_____

_____

2. Bonuses were given to new recruits joining the Continental army. Why was this a good or bad idea?

_____

_____

_____

_____

_____

3. Do you think Washington could have won at Yorktown without French help? Why?

_____

_____

_____

_____

_____

_____

Name_____ Date_____

CHALLENGES

1. Where did Washington spend the winter of 1777–1778, and where was Howe at that time?

_____

2. Why did boots captured by privateers not help Washington's men?

_____

_____

3. What arts did von Steuben teach the Continentals?

_____

_____

4. Why was Washington furious with Lee at Monmouth?

_____

_____

5. What important prisoner did George Rogers Clark capture?

_____

6. Who did the Conway Cabal support as a replacement for Washington?

_____

7. Why did Alexander Hamilton leave the army for a while?

_____

_____

8. What happened to Major Andre?

_____

_____

9. Who was known as the "Swamp Fox," and who was "Lighthorse"?

_____

10. What French officers cooperated in trapping Cornwallis at Yorktown?

_____

THE CONFEDERATION

STATES. For the states, declaring independence meant an end to colonial rule. Now they could create the kind of government that suited them. Much that happened in making state constitutions resulted from popular ideas about the role of government and the colonial experience. They believed in the contract theory: that is, governments are created by the people who write a contract (constitution) listing what government can and cannot do. They wanted a Bill of Rights to keep government from going too far. They did not trust the governors (because of their experience with royal governors), but also restricted the legislature's powers. Some states included property or religious qualifications for voting.

All of the states developed a separation of power principle, with the governor, legislature, and judges independent of each other. Governors and legislatures usually served a one-year term. In some states, the governor was elected by the people; in others, the legislature chose him.

SECOND CONTINENTAL CONGRESS. When the first delegates were chosen by the states to attend the Second Continental Congress, no one had any idea circumstances would cause them to appoint a general, raise an army and navy, borrow money, and send diplomats. They were a committee acting like a government, but without authority. John Dickinson of Pennsylvania drew up the Articles of Confederation. Congress approved them in 1777. Before they could go into effect, however, all 13 states had to approve them.

The Articles of Confederation allowed for only a weak association of states, with each state retaining its sovereignty.

The states were slow to approve the Articles. Some state leaders were so afraid of outside authority that they opposed the Articles. The Articles clearly described the proposed Confederation as a "league of friendship," and said: "Each state retains its sovereignty [self-rule], freedom and independence." There were complaints in large states like Virginia and New York because they had only one vote, no more than small states like New Hampshire. The main complaint had nothing to do with the Articles. Small seaboard states like Maryland objected to the large land claims of other states, some stretching to the Mississippi River. They wanted the states with claims to large uninhabited regions to give them up. In 1781 Virginia gave up its claims, and Maryland agreed to sign.

CONFEDERATION CONGRESS. Each state chose from two to seven delegates to sit in Congress, but no matter how many they chose, the state still had only one vote. The members were appointed and paid by their states, so they were not free to vote for anything unpopular in their states. Attendance at meetings was poor, and without delegates from nine states present, no business of importance could be done. Some delegates who were appointed never attended a session, and states sometimes did not bother to appoint any delegates.

To pay for the war, Congress had to beg the states to send their share of the cost, but the states seldom did. Congress then printed up some more Continental money, which was close to being worthless. By 1781 it took $150 of Continental notes to buy a Spanish dollar. Only loans from the French and Dutch kept the money from being worthless.

In 1783 Congress was given the happier task of approving the Treaty of Paris which ended the Revolution. Terms provided were (1) Britain recognized U.S. independence, (2) boundary lines with Canada were drawn close to where they are now, and the Mississippi River was the western border, (3) the United States could fish off Newfoundland and Nova Scotia, (4) all debts contracted between English and American citizens were still valid, (5) Congress was to recommend that states return loyalist rights and property, and (6) British forces were to leave U.S. territory "with all convenient speed."

Despite the weaknesses mentioned and those to be discussed in the next unit, Congress did make two important decisions that had great importance.

Land Ordinance of 1785. The land north and west of the Ohio River had been given to Congress by the states claiming it. Congress was anxious to sell the land to pay off Revolutionary War debts and to pay current expenses.

The "Old Northwest" was to be surveyed, and auctions were to be held in each state for surveyed land. All the land was divided into townships of six miles square (or 36 square miles). The minimum bid accepted was $1 an acre, with the land sold in 640-acre (one square mile) plots. One square mile of each township was set aside to support education.

An area of 640 acres is a reasonable-sized farm in that region today, but in that time, it was more than a farmer could plant and harvest crops on without help. The $640 minimum price also discouraged most pioneer farmers. This opened the door to speculators with money and political influence. Two major companies were formed to take advantage of the Land Ordinance: the Ohio Company and Scioto Company.

Northwest Ordinance of 1787. Few pioneers wanted to settle an area without government. In July 1787, while the Constitutional Convention was meeting, the Confederation Congress passed the Northwest Ordinance. It provided a system of governing the Old Northwest. The plan called for three phases: (1) The territory was to be governed by a governor, secretary, and three judges appointed by Congress. (2) When 5,000 free adult males settled the territory, it was to elect a two-house legislature. (3) When the population reached 60,000, it could apply for admission to the Union. It would then be the equal of all the other states. No fewer than three and no more than five states could be formed. The ordinance provided guarantees of rights and prohibited slavery (Jefferson's suggestion). Unfortunately, the Confederation is more noted for its failures than accomplishments.

Activity

Stage a session of the Confederation Congress with nine students chosen to represent states. One student should speak in favor of the Land Ordinance, but another student should be appointed to argue it is unfair to the poor. Arrange for the seven other students to vote for the Land Ordinance. Then stop the action, and ask the students what the lone opposing member should do. [Hopefully, they will advise the delegate to walk out; without nine, no quorum.]

Name_____ Date_____

POINTS TO PONDER

1. It is often said we learn from bad experiences. What were some ways states tried to avoid repeating the past?

_____

_____

_____

_____

2. If you were appointed by the legislature to attend the Confederation Congress, why might you not be overjoyed by the opportunity?

_____

_____

_____

_____

_____

3. The charge was made that the Confederation Congress favored the wealthy. Why did that opinion develop?

_____

_____

_____

_____

_____

Name_____ Date_____

CHALLENGES

1. Why did states limit the power of governors as much as they did?

_____

_____

2. How many years did most governors and legislators serve in the newly formed state governments?

_____

3. Who was the author of the Articles of Confederation?

_____

4. Why did some in New York think the voting system proposed by the Articles was unfair?

_____

_____

5. What caused Maryland to finally approve the Articles?

_____

_____

6. Apathy is a "don't care" attitude. What signs were there that delegates appointed to Congress were often apathetic?

_____

_____

7. What saved Continental dollars from becoming worthless?

_____

_____

8. How many acres are in a square mile?

_____

9. What were the two largest companies going into western land speculation?

_____

10. How many slaves were to be admitted into the Old Northwest?

_____

THE CONSTITUTIONAL CONVENTION

As leaders like Washington and Madison watched the Confederation over the years, it became obvious that its failures outweighed its successes. Out of their concerns came the call for a new constitution.

THE FAILURES. Anyone acquainted with a Continental soldier heard his complaints about Congress. He had fought the war, but was not paid until months or even years later. After Yorktown, many of the hungry soldiers headed home, bitter with Congress for neglecting them. In 1782 Washington received a letter from Colonel Lewis Nicola expressing the men's frustrations with Congress and suggesting that Washington take over as king. Washington wrote a stern reply that left no room for doubt about his position on the subject. He told Nicola

As Secretary for Foreign Affairs, John Jay negotiated the unpopular Jay-Gardoqui Treaty with Spain.

that he could not have found any man more opposed to his scheme. For the good of the country, Nicola's reputation, and respect for Washington, "banish these thoughts from your mind, and never communicate . . . a sentiment of the like nature."

Even Washington's trusted aide, Alexander Hamilton, suggested that the army was at the boiling point and said that if Washington did not take over, someone else would. Washington wrote back that he supported the soldiers in getting what they deserved, but added: "Unhappy situation this! God forbid we should ever be involved in it!" Many of those who leaned toward General Gates began whispering and sending anonymous messages about the need to demand justice from Congress. A meeting of officers at Newburgh, Pennsylvania, Washington's headquarters, was scheduled for March 15, 1783.

Washington hinted he would not attend, but during the meeting, he walked in. He reminded the officers of their patriotism and sacrifices and the natural slowness of legislatures to act. Nothing was working, but Washington remembered a letter he had received from a congressman. Taking it out, he tried to read it, but the words blurred. Putting on his glasses (which few had ever seen him wear), he apologized: "Gentlemen, you will permit me to put on my spectacles, for I have not only grown gray but also blind in the service of my country." Some officers cried, and all voted opposition to the anonymous address and vowed their confidence in Congress.

FOREIGN AFFAIRS. The United States was the only new republic on the globe, and that might have frightened Europe's kings if the new nation had not been so pathetic. It had no ruler and after 1783 had no army either. States ignored Congress whenever they chose. It was a nation falling apart. The United States was a like newborn baby, with no one volunteering to provide it with new milk.

England. John Adams was sent as minister (ambassador) to England and properly bowed to the king. He could accomplish nothing because feelings were so bitter against the

United States. The issues of debts to British citizens and loyalist property kept cropping up. His complaints about English troops on American soil and the closing of ports in the British West Indies to American ships (the United States was now a foreign nation) got nowhere.

France. Thomas Jefferson was appointed minister to France and found the job "a perfect school for humility." Louis XVI's government was in bad financial condition, and it constantly reminded Jefferson of the 35 million livres the United States owed France.

Spain. John Jay had the task of Secretary for Foreign Affairs. One of his biggest problems was Spanish threats to cut American use of the Mississippi River. For westerners without roads, the mighty river was their only way to ship goods to market. But Jay was also pressured by eastern merchants to open Spanish ports to their goods. Jay, working with the Spanish ambassador, developed the Jay-Gardoqui Treaty. It gave up the use of the river in return for the right to trade in Spanish ports. The west bitterly opposed it, as did the south. It was rejected by a 7–5 vote, two short of the number needed to be adopted.

STATES. In some states, rebellious citizens wanted government to relieve their problems. Rhode Island's legislature was taken over by debtor farmers. It began putting out nearly worthless paper money. Debtors now hunted down lenders to pay off their bills. The New Hampshire legislature was surrounded by angry farmers demanding cheap money and had to be rescued by the militia. The worst situation was in Massachusetts in 1786. Daniel Shays became the symbolic leader of rebellious farmers who wanted mortgage foreclosures stopped. Surrounding courthouses and threatening violence against judges, they controlled some counties. The militia finally restored order, but many feared the classes were turning on each other.

GATHERINGS. Some people, like Franklin, had thought for years that the colonies (and later states) should get together and talk over their differences. In 1785 Washington asked that representatives from Maryland and Virginia meet at his home and discuss problems of trade on the Potomac. The meeting went so well that delegates talked of another meeting the next year with *all* the states represented. The Annapolis Conference was disappointing; delegates from only five states attended (four states appointed delegates who did not come, and four did not appoint delegates). Hamilton and James Madison proposed that a meeting be held in Philadelphia in 1787 "for the sole purpose of revising the Articles of Confederation."

In a year filled with Shays' Rebellion, financial hard times, and reports of foreign agents trying to persuade states and influential persons to come over to their side, states realized something had to be done. When Washington decided to attend the 1787 meeting, other states realized this was going to be an important meeting, and they sent their most talented people as well.

Activity

Your class is the Confederation Congress, and you are well aware of the gathering at Philadelphia to "revise the Articles." List the revisions that are apparent to you that might be made.

119

Name_____ Date_____

POINTS TO PONDER

1. Why was the Newburgh Conspiracy so dangerous? If it had succeeded, what difference would it have made to the United States?

_____

_____

_____

_____

2. Part of British anger came because the United States got help from France. Do you think this was a legitimate complaint? Why?

_____

_____

_____

_____

_____

3. Supporters of the convention at Philadelphia were not completely honest in saying they wanted to revise the Articles. Do you think they should have plainly said they wanted to do away with the Articles?

_____

_____

_____

_____

_____

Name_____ Date_____

CHALLENGES

1. Who suggested that Washington take over as king?

_____

2. What kind of response did he receive?

_____

_____

3. What other general was there speculation about as a potential leader?

_____

4. What action by Washington stopped the Newburgh Conspiracy?

_____

_____

5. What issues stood in the way of Adams being successful in England?

_____

_____

6. Who had the "perfect school for humility"? Why was France so insistent on getting its money back?

_____

_____

7. What parts of the country opposed the Jay-Gardoqui treaty?

_____

_____

8. What state was taken over by the debtors?

_____

9. Who was credited with leading the rebellion closing Massachusetts courts?

_____

10. Who proposed calling the meeting at Philadelphia?

_____

THE CONSTITUTION THEY WROTE

Perhaps the most important gathering ever to take place on U.S. soil began on May 14, 1787. To this meeting came people like George Washington and James Madison from Virginia, Benjamin Franklin and Gouverneur Morris from Pennsylvania, Alexander Hamilton from New York, and Roger Sherman from Connecticut. The youngest delegate was Jonathan Dayton of New Jersey (26), and the oldest was Benjamin Franklin (81). The average age was 43. The 55 delegates attending were from 12 states. Rhode Island's legislature, still controlled by debtor farmers, was the lone holdout.

Delegates to the Constitutional Convention met in the Pennsylvania State House in Philadelphia.

The east room of the State House where they met looked imposing, but there were problems. It was summer; if they left the windows open, the noise from the cobblestone street and swarms of flies made concentrating impossible. They closed the windows and endured the heat. It was two weeks after the scheduled beginning before there was a quorum of seven states. The slow beginning gave delegates a chance to get acquainted and share ideas. Washington found that all realized the importance of doing something soon or "anarchy and confusion will ensue."

Washington gave a brief speech to the delegates in which he told them to work for the best document they could write. "Let us raise a standard to which the wise and honest can repair. The event is in the hands of God." While they waited, the Virginians met and drew up a plan for government calling for separation of powers and checks and balances.

The choice of Washington to be the presiding officer meant he could not speak, but his influence was strong on delegates. Many delegates knew him well; they had eaten at his table or perhaps had a long talk with him some time in the past. Washington's eagerness to accomplish great things was contagious. His face clearly showed his boredom, pleasure, or anger, and delegates studied his face during the sessions. Long-winded speakers or endless debates met an icy glare that told them it was time to stop talking; a good compromise was greeted with a smile.

The first rule they made was secrecy; not even wives were to know what went on in the Convention. The members kept their word, although there were a few minor slips. Early in the Convention, a delegate found a copy of the Virginia Plan in the lobby and gave it to Washington. He waited until the day's business was over, then held the page up, and after warning the members to be more careful, slammed it down on a desk. No one was that careless again. Benjamin Franklin's outgoing ways required that when he went out to eat, other delegates went with him. If he began discussing the Convention, they took him home.

James Madison became known as the "father of the Constitution." During the

Convention, he kept detailed records of the debates, which the official secretary of the Convention did not do. Madison sat with his back to Washington, so it was obvious what he was doing. Because of Madison's work, we have a better idea of what went on during the sessions.

VIRGINIA PLAN. Governor Edmund Randolph of Virginia took the floor on May 29 and proposed 15 resolutions. It was obvious that revision of the Articles was not on his mind. The basic provisions were: (1) a two-house legislature with the upper house chosen by the lower, (2) a "national executive" elected by the legislature, (3) a national court structure with judges chosen by the legislature. The small states were suspicious and countered with their own NEW JERSEY PLAN. Proposed by William Paterson, it is also known as the "small state" plan. It continued the Articles of Confederation, but would: (1) give Congress power to impose taxes and regulate trade, (2) create an "executive," a committee elected by Congress, and (3) have a Supreme Court appointed by the executive.

MAJOR DECISIONS. Two-house legislature. The first major sticking point was to decide how many delegates to Congress there would be. The big states wanted representation based on population; the small states wanted equality. Roger Sherman proposed what became known as the "Great Compromise," a two-house legislature. The Senate was to have an equal number of members from each state; the House was to be based on population. It was later decided that House members were to serve two-year terms, and Senators were to serve six-year terms. The executive branch was to be headed by a president with the power to appoint (subject to Senate approval) and to be commander in chief (the rules for the military and money allotted to be set by Congress). Treaties made by the president had to be approved by a two-thirds Senate vote before going into effect. The president was to be selected by an Electoral College. The judicial branch was to consist of a Supreme Court and inferior courts established by Congress. The President was to choose judges (subject to Senate approval), and they were to serve for life or during good behavior. The three independent branches worked on the idea of checks and balances.

The POWERS OF THE NATIONAL GOVERNMENT were listed in Article I, Section 8. The delegates wanted to make sure this government did not take away the rights of the states or the people. Many of the items listed have been expanded far beyond what the writers expected. The system developed was a federal system, with certain powers given to Congress and others reserved to the states. Some issues were not mentioned and became problems for the nation to wrestle with in the future.

Still, they had done well. By September, they were ready to pack their bags and head for home. In many ways, the fight ahead was to be harder because now they had to sell their product to conventions in the states.

Activity

Hold a mock Constitutional Convention with "delegates" deciding how the president should be chosen. Remind students of the differences between large and small states on this subject.

Name_____ Date_____

POINTS TO PONDER

1. The Convention was very secretive and did not want to "leak" information to newspapers about their proceedings. Why? Do you think that would be possible today?

_____

_____

_____

_____

2. How would government using the "New Jersey Plan" look different from the U.S. government of today?

_____

_____

_____

_____

3. Why did they list the powers of the national government in Article I, Section 8, rather than trust Congress and the president to do the right thing?

_____

_____

_____

_____

_____

_____

Name_____ Date_____

CHALLENGES

1. Who were the youngest and oldest delegates at the Convention?

_____

2. What were two reasons for keeping the windows closed?

_____

_____

3. How did Washington reflect his displeasure with long-winded speakers?

_____

_____

4. What delegate was most closely watched to prevent him from talking too much?

_____

5. Who is known as the "father of the Constitution"? What was unusual about the way he sat?

_____

_____

6. Who proposed the Virginia Plan to the Convention?

_____

7. Under the Virginia Plan, who was to choose the upper house?

_____

8. Who would head the government under the "small state" plan?

_____

9. Who makes rules for the military under the Constitution?

_____

10. What is a federal system?

_____

RATIFICATION AND A NEW REPUBLIC

Benjamin Franklin, America's wise patriarch, added little to the Convention, but oddly he made some of the most enduring statements regarding it. On its last day, Franklin asked another delegate to read a statement for him. It conceded that the Constitution might not be perfect, but was so close to perfection that it astonished him. He favored the Constitution because "I expect no better, and because I am not sure that it is not the best."

As they lined up to sign the Constitution, he said that throughout the Convention, he had noticed the sun carved on the back of Washington's chair. He could not tell whether it was rising or setting, "but at length I have the happiness to know that it is a rising and not a setting sun." Like Franklin, other delegates were pleased with their product, but none was happy with *all* of it. Washington saw faults but

As the Constitutional Convention concluded, Benjamin Franklin said the sun carved on Washington's chair was a rising sun, representing the rising hopes for the new nation.

knew amendments could correct them. As they started home, delegates knew the task was not done; in fact, some of the hardest work lay ahead.

THE RATIFICATION PROCESS. The writers had cleverly by-passed state legislatures; Article VII provided that ratification by conventions in nine states was sufficient for the Constitution to go into effect. The conventions were chosen for one purpose, to accept or reject the new Constitution. The "supremacy clause" (Article VI) required that state constitutions and laws, as well as federal treaties, laws, and all judicial decisions, conform to the U.S. Constitution. Therefore, nothing in it could be taken lightly. Those who liked what they saw were Federalists; those feeling it should be rejected were labelled Anti-Federalists.

FEDERALISTS included such well-known citizens as George Washington, James Madison, Alexander Hamilton, and John Jay. They were convinced that something had to be done to make the United States a true nation. Otherwise, it was going to be gobbled up by one or more European nations. Besides, they felt genuine pride in what had been accomplished. There were marks of pure genius in the safeguards the Constitution had created against arbitrary power in the hands of any government official.

ANTI-FEDERALISTS expressed many fears. Among them: (1) states were giving up too much power, (2) the taxing power was too broad, (3) debtors said states couldn't issue paper money anymore, and (4) with no bill of rights, the new government would become a tyranny like England had been. During the Convention, George Mason suggested that a Bill of Rights be added; it would quiet the people's fears and aid in getting the Constitution through state conventions. The proposal was not seriously considered for several reasons. Southerners were afraid it would mention "natural rights," and they owned slaves. State constitutions had bills of rights, and Roger Sherman argued they were not repealed by the new Constitution. Some feared that any listing of rights might leave some out, and the national government would take those away from the citizen. Besides, hastily considered additions might create new problems in getting the Constitution approved by the states.

THE RATIFYING CONVENTIONS. The Confederation Congress was unhappy that it had been ignored by the Convention, but had little choice except to submit the Constitution to the states for approval. Before the year 1787 ended, three states had approved and two more signed on in the first two weeks of January 1788. Then came Massachusetts, where Hancock was won over with the suggestion that he might become vice-president, and Samuel Adams was promised that amendments would be added to protect rights. The Bay State gave approval by a narrow 187–168 vote. New Hampshire was the ninth state, but New York and Virginia had not yet approved. They were too important for the Union to succeed without them.

James Madison led the fight for the Constitution in Virginia, where some powerful Anti-Federalists, including Patrick Henry, George Mason, and Richard Henry Lee, wanted to shelve it. Madison soon became aware of a variety of fears the opposition had raised. His solution to persuade those who had doubts about whether rights were secure with this new Constitution was to promise that a Bill of Rights would be added by amendment when Congress met. The vote was 89–79 in favor.

In New York, Alexander Hamilton faced Governor George Clinton's tough opposition. The two men didn't like each other, and Washington had to caution Hamilton not to make this a battle of personalities. Sometime in October 1788, Hamilton met with Madison and John Jay to discuss writing a series of articles they called *The Federalist*. All articles were signed "Publius," but it is generally believed Hamilton wrote about 50, Madison about 30, and Jay (who had serious health problems) only five. They explained why the Confederation was not working and how the Constitution was going to remedy the problems. It has since become a classic in political science and a good guide to the thinking of the founding fathers. Even with their good work, the Constitution passed by a narrow margin of only 30–27.

The 11 states that had approved the Constitution chose the electors who picked George Washington as president and John Adams as vice president. The state legislatures selected their senators, and the people elected their first representatives. The new government was on its way

North Carolina and Rhode Island held out. The Tar-heel state finally approved in November 1789, after Washington had begun his first term as president. Stubborn Rhode Island approved May 29, 1790, by a vote of 34–32. Benjamin Franklin had been asked what kind of government they had created; he replied: "A republic, sir, if we can keep it."

Activity

Looking at the arguments given by Anti-Federalists to oppose the Constitution, how would the Federalists in the class try to convince them that they had nothing to fear?

Name_____ Date_____

POINTS TO PONDER

1. What did Franklin's remark about the rising and setting sun mean?

_____

_____

_____

_____

_____

2. In what ways did Federalists have the advantage over Anti-Federalists?

_____

_____

_____

_____

_____

_____

3. Look at some modern problems between states and the federal government. If the Constitution were up for reapproval, what changes might the states want to make?

_____

_____

_____

_____

_____

_____

_____

Name_____ Date_____

CHALLENGES

1. How did Washington think improvements would be made in the Constitution?

_____

_____

2. Who in the states was to approve or disapprove the Constitution?

_____

3. What clause requires that all laws conform to the Constitution?

_____

4. What did Federalists fear?

_____

_____

5. Who wanted a Bill of Rights to quiet people's fears?

_____

6. How many states approved the Constitution in 1787?

_____

7. How was Hancock persuaded to support it?

_____

_____

8. Who were some powerful Anti-Federalists in Virginia?

_____

_____

9. Who were the authors of *The Federalist?*

_____

_____

10. Who chose the first senators?

_____

Name _____ Date _____

COLONIAL TIMES CROSSWORD PUZZLE

Use the clues below to complete the puzzle. All answers come from the narrative pages.

ACROSS

1. He labelled the incident in Boston a "horrible massacre." (two words)
9. Patriots dressed as Indians dumped the cargo of several ships at the _____ _____ _____.
13. The Declaration of _____ was written by Jefferson and stated the colonists' wish to be free.
15. Colony with many Quaker settlers
17. This proposed a two-house legislature with an executive and judges chosen by the legislature. (two words)
18. Articles written to promote ratifying the Constitution (two words)
19. Document the U.S. government is based on; written in 1787
20. Patriotic pamphlet written by Thomas Paine (two words)

DOWN

2. Ship that brought the Pilgrims to Plymouth
3. Favored English rule
4. Place in Massachusetts noted for witchcraft trials
5. Washington's professional army
6. Required colonists to buy revenue stamps to place on all legal documents (two words)
7. Contracted themselves to work, usually for seven years, for whoever would pay their way to America (two words)
8. Those who supported independence
10. The "Lost Colony"
11. The first fighting in the Revolution took place at _____ and Concord.
12. Organization formed to protest the Stamp Act and boycott British goods (three words)
14. Hero of Ticonderoga and Saratoga who later turned traitor (two words)
16. Colony established in 1607 on the Virginia coast

ANSWER KEYS

The First Inhabitants of North America (page 5)
1. Scandinavians: Leif Ericson.
2. Signs: large structures and calendars.
3. Amerinds: anthropologists.
4. Language: Algonquin.
5. Lakes: Iroquois.
6. Tribe: Pequot.
7. Symbol: animal or totem.
8. Ponce: didn't like him and attacked him.
9. De Soto: used hunting dogs on them, burned villages, took hostages, took them in chain gangs.
10. Descendant: razorback hog.

France and England Arrive (page 9)
1. Cartier: New France.
2. Champlain: killed two Iroquois warriors.
3. Utopia: ideal society.
4. Goals: expand trade, increase markets, reduce unemployment.
5. Supplies: war with Spain [including Battle of Spanish Armada].
6. Jamestown: King James I.
7. Smith: Opechancanough
8. Smith's life: Pocahontas.
9. Crop: tobacco.
10. Institutions: slavery and democracy.

Plymouth and Massachusetts Bay (page 13)
1. Puritan: wanted to purify Anglican church.
2. Separatist: wanted to separate from Anglican church.
3. Effect: made them more stubborn.
4. Governor: William Bradford.
5. Name: Council of New England.
6. Holiday: Thanksgiving.
7. Morton: traded guns and liquor, danced and sang around May Pole.
8. Detail: no mention of where meetings were to be held.
9. Food: game and fish available.
10. Languages: Greek and Latin.

New Colonies Planted in the North (page 17)
1. Royal: king.
2. Charter: elected.
3. Connecticut: charter.
4. Hooker: the people.
5. Williams: disagreed on too many subjects with leaders.
6. Mason: Anglican farmers and fishermen.
7. Minuit: bought Manhattan Island for $24 (60 guilders).
8. New Jersey: George Carteret and Lord Berkeley.
9. Pennsylvania: Quakers.
10. Delaware: had same governor as Pennsylvania.

Settling the Southern Colonies (page 21)
1. Group: Roman Catholics.
2. Quit-rent: Lord Baltimore.
3. Act: No. Didn't believe in divinity of Jesus Christ.
4. Charleston: had straight streets.
5. South Carolina: rice.
6. Colony: South Carolina.
7. North Carolina: tobacco and corn.
8. Reputation: drew outlaws and runaways.
9. Oglethorpe: inmates of debtors' prisons and German Protestants.
10. Group: slaves.

Religion in the Colonies (page 25)
1. Europe: heretics and disloyal.
2. B's: could leave country or form own colony.
3. New York: Dutch Reformed and Anglican.
4. South: Anglican.
5. Common: both wanted freedom of religion.
6. Mood: bad; colony had many problems.
7. Total: 175.
8. Deist: no, believed God wasn't concerned.
9. Sermon: "Sinners in the Hands of an Angry God."
10. Log College: William Tennent.

The Colonial Economy (page 29)
1. P: Pauper, person who wouldn't work.
2. Homes: brick walls and tile roof.
3. Swedes: log cabins.
4. Tools: hoes, sickles, and flails.
5. Tips: thought iron poisoned the soil.
6. Frontier: hogs walked to market.
7. South: tobacco, rice, and indigo.
8. Boston: 1,600 ships.
9. Navigation Acts: restrict sale of colonial products.
10. Tavern: bad food, bad sleeping conditions, no privacy.

Social Status in the Colonies (page 33)
1. Rank: nobility; part of royal family.
2. Example: minister.
3. Goody: middle class.
4. Jim: unskilled worker, indentured, apprentice, free black, or slave.
5. Boston: Lodge.
6. Indenture: 5–7 years.
7. Group: apprentices.
8. Slaves: 5,000.
9. Crops: rice and tobacco.
10. New England: farmers had such small holdings that they didn't need slaves.

Slavery in the Colonies (page 37)
1. Africans: bound servants.
2. Marylanders: afraid that if slaves were Christians, they would have to be freed.
3. Georgians: saw wealth of other slave-holders.
4. Changes: Royal Adventurers supplied 3,000 slaves a year to America; West Indian planters sold slaves to America; more slave women came to America, thus more slave births.
5. Declaration: talked about all men being equal and having rights and deserving freedom.
6. Rights: life, liberty, pursuit of happiness.
7. Who: everyone (all men).
8. Escape: offered freedom by Dunmore for fighting.
9. Slavery: no.
10. Trade: South Carolina and Georgia.

Young People's Lives in the Colonies (page 41)
1. Half-brothers: because so many women died in childbirth.
2. Worry: 20 years old.
3. Activities: fire brigades, militia, church groups.
4. Girls: quilting bees, church socials, garden groups.
5. Hunting: both fun and provided food.
6. Huzzlecap: pitching pennies.
7. Hired: musical ability.
8. Ballad: "Springfield Mountain."
9. Critic: Increase Mather.
10. Actors: Lewis Hallam and David Douglas.

Colonial Clothing (page 45)
1. Families: made it; it was cheaper and English goods weren't as readily available.
2. Change: very slowly, noticeably every 10–30 years (depending on time).
3. Styles: watched what newcomers wore, read letters from European friends and family, looked at fashion plates and fashion babies.
4. Babies: one-foot dolls wearing the newest styles that were circulated through Europe and America.
5. Clothes: grow and harvest raw goods, spin them, weave them, sew by hand.
6. Boys: wore skirts until 5 years old.
7. Pockets: not sewn into skirt, very large.
8. Minimum: count may vary; should be around 10.
9. Maximum: count may vary; should be close to 20.
10. Religion: women wore aprons, kerchiefs, and caps even though they weren't in style.

The New Man (and Woman) (page 49)
1. Book: *Letters from an American Farmer.*
2. Later writer: Alexis de Tocqueville.
3. Voyage: made him realize he was never going back.
4. Disadvantage: could only blame it on himself.
5. Failure: Americans accepted failures, but not those who didn't try.
6. Phips: Maine frontiersman to Massachusetts royal governor.
7. Abilities: with ax and Pennsylvania rifle.
8. Divine right: ruler appointed by God; those disagreeing were wrong and evil.
9. Artists: John Copley and Benjamin West.
10. Greatness: Michael Wigglesworth, Anne Bradstreet, Dr. Benjamin Rush, and Benjamin Franklin.

The Head Under the Crown (page 53)
1. James I: closest living relative of Elizabeth I.
2. Left: Puritans.
3. Cavaliers supported king; Roundheads supported Parliament.
4. Relatives: Washington, Jefferson, Henry, and Randolph.
5. Ruled: Oliver and Richard Cromwell.
6. Group: Jews.
7. Charles II: took bribe from French.
8. Relationship: William son-in-law, Mary was daughter.
9. Bill: couldn't be Catholic.
10. George I: Elector of Hanover.

Government in the Colonies (page 57)
1. Obey: Thomas Hobbes.
2. Life, liberty and property: John Locke.
3. Lords: Council.
4. Colonies: Rhode Island and Connecticut.
5. Governors: No. Owed job to king.
6. Proprietary: had to, or king would make it royal colony.
7. Lower houses: upper class.
8. Appeals: Council.
9. Discourage: withhold all or part of his pay.
10. Journalist: John Peter Zenger.

New France (page 61)
1. Power: the king.
2. Sovereign Council: made laws until king's regulations arrived, and was supreme court.
3. Responsible: intendant.
4. Laval: brandy trade.
5. Priests: tortured and killed.
6. Organization: Company of One Hundred Associates.
7. Ages: 16 for women, 20 for men.
8. Reward: 400 livres.
9. Coureurs: wild and corrupted Indians.
10. Combined: 3,200.

Wars Come to North America (page 65)
1. Frontenac: led them in war dance.
2. Dustin: killed and scalped 10 of captors.
3. Deerfield: was attacked. 50 killed and 111 captured.
4. Outpost: New Orleans.
5. Louisbourg: had taken it from professional soldiers.
6. Washington: to inform French they were trespassing on Virginia soil.
7. Name: Fort Necessity.
8. Who: William Pitt.
9. Duquesne: John Forbes.
10. Generals: Montcalm and Wolfe.

Beginnings of Conflict (1763–66) (page 69)

1. Pontiac: Detroit and Fort Pitt.
2. Proclamation Line: satisfy British fur merchants and reduce chance of another uprising.
3. Grenville: from English and colonial taxpayers.
4. Navigation Acts: to limit what could be shipped and who could ship it.
5. Document: allowed customs collectors to search anywhere for smuggled goods; search warrant.
6. Smuggler: Admiralty Court [court conducted by naval officers].
7. Merchants: refused to buy British products.
8. Stamp Tax: direct tax on Americans not represented in Parliament.
9. Critics: James Otis and Patrick Henry.
10. Declaratory: said Parliament had every right to pass any law they wished to regulate colonies.

New Taxes and a Massacre (1767–70) (page 73)

1. Riot: a liberty pole.
2. Chancellor: Secretary of Treasury.
3. Taxes: external collected before item is shipped.
4. Taxes: glass, paint, lead, paper, and tea.
5. Parliament: too few and too costly to make it worthwhile.
6. *Romney:* to help customs collectors.
7. *Liberty:* John Hancock.
8. 92: resistance.
9. *Liberty:* government finally gave up prosecution.
10. Lawyer: John Adams.

George III & Company (page 77)

1. George I: No, signed bills without question.
2. Title: Elector of Hanover.
3. Control: the Queen.
4. Relationship: grandson.
5. Why: Lord North did whatever he asked.
6. Title: prime minister.
7. Officers: Amherst and Keppel.
8. Germain: had been court-martialed for cowardice.
9. Sandwich: ate meat between pieces of bread.
10. Barrington: "wickedest herd that ever good men served under."

Adams, Henry, & Paine (page 81)

1. Office: Boston treasurer.
2. Caucus Club: political group.
3. Bernard: celebrated with bonfires and roaring cannons.
4. Arrest: too popular.
5. Issue: Stamp Act.
6. Help: France, Spain, and Holland.
7. Quote: "Give me liberty or give me death."
8. Introduction: Benjamin Franklin.
9. Pamphlet: Common Sense.
10. Sales: 120,000.

Boston's Tea Party (1771–1774) (page 85)
1. North: to prove England was strong.
2. Hancock: someone voted against him.
3. *Gaspee:* Lt. Dudingston.
4. Tea tax: no, to help East India Company.
5. Resistance: New York and Philadelphia smugglers/businessmen.
6. Sold: none.
7. Hutchinson: had financial stake in it.
8. Washington: feared England might overreact.
9. Boston: Boston Port Act.
10. Replaced: General Thomas Gage.

Declaring Independence (1774–1776) (page 89)
1. "I" word: independence; afraid it would scare off southerners.
2. Boucher: wouldn't like each other; Henry wanted independence.
3. Galloway: "grand council"; had power to accept or reject acts of Parliament before they became law in the colonies.
4. Intolerable: violated colonists' rights.
5. Association: block merchants from selling British-made goods.
6. Trouble: on their way back to Boston.
7. Montreal: French Canadians not interested in joining colonists.
8. Nickname: Hessians.
9. Proposed: Richard Henry Lee (Virginia)
10. Committee: <u>Jefferson</u>, Adams, and Franklin.

Washington: Symbol of the Revolution (page 93)
1. Responsibility: take care of mother and 4 brothers and sisters.
2. Rules: 110.
3. Military: Half-brother Lawrence.
4. Plantation: Mt. Vernon.
5. Role: covered retreat.
6. Name: Martha Custis.
7. Slaves: 200; thought it was a poor way to get work done.
8. War: after First Continental Congress.
9. Wore: uniform of Virginia militia.
10. Informed: spy network.

Weighing the Odds (page 97)
1. Help: France and Spain.
2. War: public tired of paying for wars.
3. Enlisted: prisons, bars, and lower class neighborhoods.
4. Musket: 7 commands; 100 yards.
5. Quality: experience and training.
6. Militia: for defense of state, family, and property.
7. When: after Saratoga.
8. Radical patriots: wanted social revolution making everyone equal.
9. Loyalists: wore forest green uniforms.
10. Weapon: Pennsylvania or Kentucky rifle.

Early Stages of the War (1776–1777) (page 101)

1. Washington: New York.
2. Carleton: slowed by Arnold on Lake Champlain.
3. Clinton: loyalists not there to help him.
4. Trenton: in cold weather on Christmas Day.
5. Opportunity: Cornwallis.
6. Germain: Albany.
7. Philadelphia: rebel capital.
8. Arnold: Hon Yost.
9. Bridges: too many cannons and supply wagons.
10. Generals: Daniel Morgan, Henry Dearborn, and Benedict Arnold.

The Diplomatic War (page 105)

1. Foreign minister: Vergennes; hated England.
2. Spain: Battle of Spanish Armada (1588).
3. Reluctant: Spain's colonies might revolt.
4. Diplomats: Arthur Lee and Silas Deane.
5. Scientists: work with electricity, bifocals, and his stove.
6. Hortalez: military supplies to United States.
7. Wentworth: persuade Franklin to accept dominion status.
8. Amity and Commerce: opened trade between United States and France [by offering the treaty, France was recognizing United States as independent].
9. Fight: until United States was free.
10. De Grasse: sailed to Yorktown.

The Naval War (page 109)

1. Merchant ships: naval ship's crew divided booty.
2. Invasion: Lake Ontario and Lake Champlain.
3. Ships of line: three decks of guns.
4. Cannon: could fire 42 pound ball.
5. *La Marine*: Duc de Choiseul.
6. Ships: *Alfred* and *Columbus.*
7. Privateer: *Rattlesnake.*
8. Jones: *Ranger.*
9. Battle: *Bonhomme Richard* and *Serapis.*
10. French fleet: De Grasse.

The Road to Yorktown (page 113)

1. 1777–1778: Washington at Valley Forge, Howe at Philadelphia.
2. Boots: stored away until they mildewed.
3. Von Steuben: drilling and fighting.
4. Monmouth: Lee ordered retreat.
5. Prisoner: Henry Hamilton.
6. Conway Cabal: Horatio Gates.
7. Hamilton: angry because Washington had criticized him for being late.
8. Andre: was hanged.
9. Who: "Swamp Fox" Francis Marion; "Lighthorse" Harry Lee.
10. French: Rochambeau and de Grasse.

The Confederation (page 117)
1. Governors: bad experience with royal governors.
2. Terms: 1 year.
3. Articles: John Dickinson.
4. New York: only got one vote.
5. Maryland: Virginia gave up claims to western lands.
6. Apathy: some never attended meetings.
7. Continentals: loans from France and Holland.
8. Mile: 640 acres.
9. Land: Scioto and Ohio Companies.
10. Slavery: none.

The Constitutional Convention (page 121)
1. King: Colonel Lewis Nicola.
2. Response: absolute no.
3. Speculation: General Horatio Gates.
4. Action: put on glasses.
5. Issues: loyalist property and collection of debts.
6. School: Jefferson; France was broke.
7. Opposed: south and west.
8. Debtors: Rhode Island.
9. Rebellion: Daniel Shays.
10. Philadelphia: Madison and Hamilton.

The Constitution They Wrote (page 125)
1. Delegates: Jonathan Dayton and Benjamin Franklin.
2. Windows: noise and flies.
3. Displeasure: glared at them.
4. Talker: Benjamin Franklin.
5. Father: Madison; sat with back to Washington.
6. Virginia Plan: Edmund Randolph.
7. Upper house: chosen by lower house.
8. Head: "the executive."
9. Military: Congress.
10. Federal: gives certain powers to Congress and others reserved to states.

Ratification and a New Republic (page 129)
1. Washington: through amendments.
2. States: conventions.
3. Clause: supremacy (Article VI).
4. Federalists: Europeans would gobble them up.
5. Bill of Rights: George Mason.
6. States: three.
7. Hancock: suggested he might be named vice-president.
8. Virginia: Patrick Henry, George Mason, and Richard H. Lee.
9. Authors: Jay, Hamilton, and Madison.
10. Senators: state legislatures.

Colonial Times Crossword Puzzle (page 130)

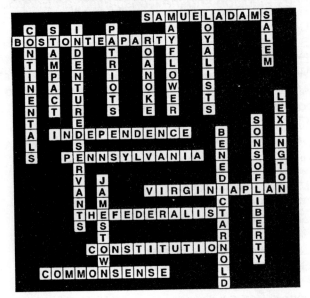

BIBLIOGRAPHY

There are many fine books on colonial and Revolutionary America. To learn more about any individual, region, or event, the student should start in an encyclopedia, and then note the sources the article's author recommends. Go to those books and look at their bibliographies. That way, you can find where even more information can be found.

This bibliography does not list every book available, but it is a beginning point for the student interested in further research.

Encyclopedias
Encyclopedia of Colonial and Revolutionary America. New York: Facts on File, 1990.
Encyclopedia of the North American Colonies. New York: Charles Scribner's: 1993.
James Madison and the Constitution: an Encyclopedia. New York: Simon & Schuster, 1994.

Colonial America
American Heritage History of the Thirteen Colonies. New York: American Heritage, 1967.
Andrews, Charles. *The Colonial Period of American History.* New Haven: Yale University, 1937.
Becker, Carl. *Beginnings of the American People.* Ithaca, NY: Cornell University, 1963.
Boland, Charles. *They All Discovered America.* New York: Pocketbooks, 1963.
Colonial America. New York: Macmillan, 1977.
Colonial Times. Worthington, Ohio: SRA, 1985.
Craven, Wesley. *The Southern Colonies in the Seventeenth Century.* Baton Rouge: Louisiana State University, 1949.
Crevecouer, Hector. *Letters from an American Farmer.* New York: NAL, 1963.
DeVoto, Bernard. *The Course of Empire.* Boston: Houghton Mifflin, 1952.
Ferling, John. *A Wilderness of Miseries: War and Warriors in Early America.* Westport, Connecticut: Greenwood, 1980.
Hakim, Joy. *A History of the United States: From Colonies to Country.* New York: Oxford University Press, 1993.
Hofstadter, Richard. *America at 1750.* New York: Knopf, 1971.
Labaree, Benjamin. *America's Nation Time: 1607–1789.* New York: Norton, 1976.
McInnis, Edgar. *Canada: a Political and Social History.* Toronto: Holt, Rinehart & Winston, 1969.
Middleton, Richard. *Colonial America: A History, 1607–1760.* Cambridge, Massachusetts: Blackwell, 1992.
Sauer, Carl. *Sixteenth Century North America.* Berkeley: University of California, 1971.
Thwaites, Reuben. *The Colonies 1492–1750.* New York: Longmans, Green, 1896.
Wertenbaker, Thomas. *The Founding of American Civilization: The Middle Colonies.* New York: Cooper Square, 1963.
Wright, Louis. *Cultural Life of the American Colonies: 1607–1763.* New York: Harper, 1957.

Pre-Revolutionary America (1763–1775)
Campbell, Norine. *Patrick Henry: Patriot and Statesman.* Santa Cruz, California: Devin, 1969.
Howard, George. *Preliminaries of the Revolution, 1763–1775.* New York: AMS, 1905.
Miller, John. *Sam Adams: Pioneer in Propaganda.* Stanford, California: Stanford University, 1936.
Morgan, Edmund. *The Birth of the Republic, 1763–1789.* Chicago: University of Chicago, 1992.
Morse, John. *John Adams.* New York: AMS, 1898.
Paine, Thomas. *The Life and Works of Thomas Paine.* New Rochelle, NY: Thomas Paine Historical Association, 1925.

Rossiter, Clinton. *The First American Revolution: The American Colonies on the Eve of Independence.* San Diego: Harcourt, Brace, 1956.

Thomas, Peter. *Tea Party to Independence.* Oxford: Oxford University, 1991.

Zobel, Hiller. *The Boston Massacre.* New York: Norton, 1970.

Revolutionary America (1776–1783)

Alden, John. *A History of the American Revolution.* New York: Da Capo, 1989.

_____, *George Washington: A Biography.* Baton Rouge: LSU, 1984.

American Heritage History of the American Revolution. New York: American Heritage, 1958.

Black, Jeremy. *War for America.* New York: St. Martin's, 1991.

Cornog, Evan. *Come All You Gallant Heroes: The World of the Revolutionary Soldier.* New York: Fraunces Tavern: 1991.

The Declaration of Independence and the Constitution. Lexington, Massachusetts: Heath, 1976.

Ferguson, E. James. *The American Revolution: A General History, 1763–1790.* Homewood, Illinois: Dorsey, 1974.

Flexner, James. *Washington, the Indispensable Man.* Boston: Little Brown, 1974.

Langguth, A.J. *Patriots: The Men Who Started the American Revolution.* New York: Simon and Schuster, 1988.

Middlekauff, *The Glorious Cause.* New York: Oxford University, 1982.

Mintz, Max. *The Generals of Saratoga: John Burgoyne and Horatio Gates.* New Haven, Connecticut: Yale, 1990.

Padover, Saul. *Jefferson.* New York: NAL, 1952.

Preston, John. *Revolution 1776.* New York: Washington Square, 1961.

Tuchman, Barbara. *The First Salute.* New York: Knopf, 1988.

Building a Nation (1783–1789)

Anderson, Thornton. *Creating the Constitution: The Convention of 1787 and the First Congress.* University Park: Pennsylvania State University, 1993.

Bowen, Catherine. *Miracle at Philadelphia.* Boston: Little, Brown, 1966.

Burns, James. *The Vineyard of Liberty: The American Experiment.* New York: Knopf, 1982.

Collier, Christopher and James. *The Constitutional Convention of 1787.* New York: Ballantine, 1986.

Flexner, James. *George Washington: the Indispensable Man.* New York: NAL Dutton, 1984.

Jensen, Merrill. *The New Nation: A History of the United States During the Confederation, 1781–1789.* New York: Knopf, 1950.

Kelly, Alfred and Winfred Haribosn. *The American Constitution: Its Origins and Development.* New York: Norton, 1976.

McDonald, Forrest. *The Formation of the American Republic.* Baltimore: Penguin, 1965.

Morris, Richard. *Witnesses at the Creation.* New York: New American Library, 1985.

Mitchell, Broadus. *Alexander Hamilton: A Concise Biography.* New York: Oxford, 1976.

Rossiter, Clinton. *1787: The Grand Convention.* New York: Macmillan, 1966.

Van Doren, Carl. *The Great Rehearsal.* New York: Viking, 1948.

Wood, Gordon. *The Creation of the American Republic, 1776–1787.* Chapel Hill: University of North Carolina, 1969.